AURA GARDEN GUIDES

Diane Jones

Conifers and Heathers

D1434187

AURA BOOKS

Aura Garden Guides

Conifers and Heathers

Diane Jones

© 1998 Advanced Marketing (UK) Ltd.,
Bicester, England

Produced by:
Transedition Limited for
Aura Books, Bicester
and first published in 2002

Editing by:
Asgard Publishing Services, Leeds

Typesetting by:
Organ Graphic, Abingdon

Picture Credits
All photographs by Bert Jones
except: Daphne and Maurice
Everett 12 (bottom); Heather
Society 74 (top, bottom right),
75; Albert Julian 79.
All drawings by Frieda Garrett:
14, 23, 28, 29, 30.

10 9 8 7 6 5 4 3 2
Printed in Dubai

ISBN 1 903938 01 5

Diane Jones' interest in heathers began in the late 1960s, inspired by John Letts' garden at Windlesham, Surrey. In 1970 she and her husband Bert moved to Somerset and began to develop a half-acre garden. Its alkaline soil influenced their choice of plants, and led to an increasing interest in conifers as well as heathers, both being evergreen and suitable for year-round display. The Pygmy Pinetum at Devizes, Wiltshire, was their inspiration in developing a fine display of conifers.

They started a small nursery business in 1974, specialising in heathers. Their range of plants has broadened as their knowledge has deepened, and now includes summer-flowering species and hybrids as well as the winter- and spring-flowering heathers that do best in alkaline conditions.

Diane Jones is currently Vice-President of the Heather Society, and Bert Jones is International Registrar for Heathers. Diane is especially interested in garden design and giving her customers advice on how best to prepare and plant their sites. Since the early 1980s she has been lecturing on heathers and garden design to local groups and within the Heather Society.

CONTENTS

What are conifers and heathers?

Conifers and heathers make very good companions in the garden — but botanically speaking, they are not very closely related.

Conifers are usually large evergreen trees. Their flowers are small, primitive, and usually insignificant. Gardeners use the term 'conifer' to cover all the living orders (except Ephedra) of the class Pinopsida (Gymnospermae). This is the class of plants with 'naked' ovules, meaning that they are not contained in ovaries. There are about 800 species, grouped in families and genera, adapted to growing in most parts of the world.

It may be worth noting in passing that only three of these species — *Juniperus communis* (the common juniper), *Pinus sylvestris* (the Scots pine) and *Taxus baccata* (the yew) — are native to the UK.

Two of the conifer species from North America — *Sequoia sempervirens* and *Sequoiadendron giganteum* — have provided the largest living organisms the world has ever known. Yet nursery growers have selected many of the plants commonly used in gardens today specifically for their dwarf habit.

All heathers are evergreen flowering shrubs of the order Magnoliopsida and the family Ericaceae. They are classified into five genera: *Andromeda, Bruckenthalia, Calluna, Daboecia* and *Erica*. The International Registration Authority for these genera is the Heather Society.

In this book we shall discuss only the 20 or so species and hybrids found in Western Europe, the adjacent islands and the Mediterranean. These are usually called 'hardy heathers', and will survive outdoors in most parts of UK.

There are a further 750 or so tender species and hybrids of *Erica* from southern Africa. A few of these are sometimes

Sequoiadendron giganteum

Heathers growing in the wild

offered in florists' shops as indoor plants.

Until quite recently, all the available garden heathers (cultivars) were selected from natural variations found either in the wild or in cultivation. Some of the plants appearing now have been carefully bred to achieve certain specific characteristics.

Why deal with both in the same book?

Despite the botanical differences between conifers and heathers, both consist of mainly evergreen trees or shrubs, and can therefore be used for similar purposes in the garden. Indeed, they are grown together in some gardens.

However, since they grow at different speeds and their final sizes can also be very different, careful thought at the design stage is very important if you

Conifers and heathers offer a wide variety of shapes and foliage colours in the garden.

want your garden to remain attractive and well balanced as it matures.

Why grow conifers and heathers?

These two groups of plants provide a wide range of heights and shapes that can lend considerable interest to the garden. Their foliage can add to that interest, offering a range of colours and textures that will carry on throughout the year.

In conifers the foliage colours range from yellows, through every shade of green, to greys, blues and even the purple winter coat of *Cryptomeria japonica* or *Thuja orientalis* 'Rosedalis'.

The range is even greater among the heathers, with creams and oranges, winter reds and brilliant new spring growth on some cultivars. Heathers also have attractive flowers in shades from white, through pink, to the deepest reds and purples. With a judicious choice of species, you can keep a floral heather display going all the year round.

Most of these plants are easy to grow. Once established, they need very little maintenance, and they are effective weed-smotherers.

Heathers live for a long time, which makes them a good investment. A large specimen, or a grafted shrub, may seem expensive when you buy it — but just think of the years of beauty it can give you!

The classification and naming of plants

The scientific naming of plants is controlled by the *International Code of Botanical Nomenclature 1994*. They are classified into a hierarchical series of groups, or *taxa*. Plants in any group share a number of characteristics. As you move down the ladder, the number of shared characteristics increases. Any plant may be placed in a number of groups. In order, those groups are:

Kingdom (*regnum*)
Division (*divisio* or *phylum*)
Class (*classis*)
Order (*ordo*)
Family (*familia*)
Tribe (*tribus*)
Genus (*genus*)
Section (*sectio*)
Series (*series*)
Species (*species*)
Variety (*varietas*)
Form (*forma*)

The plant varieties that are grown in gardens have been selected by gardeners. They are called **cultivars**. The naming of cultivars is controlled by the *International Code of Nomenclature for Cultivated Plants 1995*.

Most plants can be uniquely identified by giving their **genus** (e.g. *Juniperus*) and their **species** (e.g. *squamata*), and (for a cultivated plant) the **cultivar name** (e.g. 'Blue Star') — giving the full scientific name *Juniperus squamata* 'Blue Star'.

However, the groups, or *taxa*, above the genus are useful for showing how different plants are related to each other. The sections describing individual conifers give the **family** (e.g. Cupressaceae) to which each genus belongs. As all the heathers belong to the family Ericaceae, in this case the **subfamily** (e.g. Arbutoideae) is given.

Where to use conifers and heathers

Like so much else in gardening, this is very much a matter of personal taste, and your choice is limited only by your own imagination.

Beds

When you're planning and planting beds, the architectural qualities of conifers and the taller heathers will provide structure and balance. There are times when we all admire an especially fine specimen, or a particularly attractive group. They may appeal to us because of their shape, texture, colour or setting.

Possible uses for conifers and heathers

	Conifers	Heathers
In beds	✓	✓
As specimens	✓	tall species
Among other shrubs	✓	✓
Ground cover	some cultivars	✓
Background plantings	✓	tall species
Shelter belts	hardiest species	✗
Rock gardens	✓	✓
Hedges	✓	tall species
Topiary	✓	✗
Knot gardens	✗	✓
Window boxes and tubs	true miniatures	✓
Hanging baskets	✗	✓
Bonsai	✓	tall species

When planting conifers, it's important to estimate how much space each tree will eventually occupy — take this group of mature conifers in Windsor Great Park.

The space you can allocate to a planting will determine the sizes and numbers of plants that you can use. When you're choosing conifers you need to be aware of their likely final size. The labels will normally give you the height and spread measurements after ten years' growth and at 25 years' growth (ultimate height). However, many species will live much longer, and continue to grow!

Don't forget about raised beds. These beds are often used to complement buildings, though they can equally well be garden features in their own right. They're a boon to some handicapped gardeners, bringing the plants easily within their reach — and both conifers and heathers can be grown in this way.

7

This large conifer planted in grass needs plenty of space to be seen to best advantage.

A single plant or specimen used as a feature in a planting can look particularly attractive if its shape, texture or colour contrasts nicely with the surroundings. Conifers and taller heathers can both look equally stunning if you display them in this way. Take care to select the taller specimen for its ultimate size, which should be significantly taller than the surrounding plants.

With other shrubs

Planting conifers and heathers among other shrubs will ensure variety and interest throughout the year. As both are evergreen, this may be an important feature. Some of the taller, more tender heathers will benefit from this kind of planting, which can help to protect them from the wind on open sites.

Ground cover

Conifers that are used for ground cover will normally spread more slowly than heathers. However, the rate of growth of both types of plant will depend on factors such as the chosen species, light or heavy soil, and the amount of available water.

You can achieve good ground cover both with conifers and with heathers. If you want to cover a sunny area of the garden quickly, heathers are

As specimens

A single specimen of a larger-growing conifer is often best planted on its own, in grass, to give it enough space to spread and mature. This will allow people to appreciate the full beauty of its shape. We can be grateful that our Victorian fore-

bears used this planting method, as they have left us many fine examples of large conifers. If you're planting a tree or shrub in grass, you should keep a circle of ground around the trunk clean and weed-free. To help, you can mulch this area with coarse bark.

the best solution. If you plant standard-size heathers from 3.5-in (9-cm) pots spaced 18 in (45 cm) apart, they will cover the ground in three to four years. This is an average — the rate of growth will depend on your choice of plants, your soil and the climatic conditions. Most low and medium-growing heathers are suitable for this kind of planting.

Conifers can be used for ground cover in sun or shade. Those used for ground cover (normally the prostrate and semi-prostrate kinds) will take from 10 to 20 years to reach maturity. While the young plants are becoming established, you can mulch the

Prostrate or semi-prostrate conifers make excellent ground cover plants. This one is a Juniperus squamata *'Blue Carpet'.*

space they will grow into, or plant it up with faster-growing species that can be taken out as the conifers mature.

The prostrate and semi-prostrate species of juniper seem the automatic choice for ground-cover conifers. However, there are other genera, including yew, which offer suitable species and cultivars.

Background planting

Background plantings are very effective as a 'backdrop' to the whole garden, or to particular

sections. Indeed, this is a very good way to grow conifers and heathers in the same garden. Keeping the heathers in the foreground beds and the conifers in the background solves the problem of differing growth rates.

Conifers take some time to reach their desired height. However, some of the taller shrub heathers can produce a good background, growing about 6 ft 6 in (2 m) tall in five to seven years.

As shelter belts

On some exposed sites you may want to protect your garden from the prevailing wind by planting a screen of

9

tall-growing conifers on the windward side. You will find suitable plants among the cultivars of *Chamaecyparis lawsoniana*, ×*Cupressocyparis leylandii* (Leyland cypress), *Picea omorika, Pinus nigra* or *Thuja plicata*. ×*Cupressocyparis leylandii* will need to be pruned while it's young to ensure dense growth — but it does grow very quickly.

Hedges

Because conifers are evergreen they make ideal hedges. Use them to obtain privacy, to hide unsightly objects or unappealing views, to divide a large garden into separate sections, or simply to mark boundaries.

If you want a hedge that will be at least 6 ft (1.8 m) tall, your best choice is probably ×*Cupressocyparis leylandii* (Leyland cypress) or *Thuja plicata*. The Leyland cypress will grow faster, and you can create an attractive hedge by using alternate blocks of the green species plants and one of the gold-foliage clones 'Castlewellan', 'Gold Rider' or 'Robinson's Gold'.

For a lower hedge *Taxus baccata* seems the obvious choice, but you could also use *Chamaecyparis lawsoniana, Tsuga canadensis, T. heterophylla, Thuja occidentalis* and maybe some other species.

To make a formal hedge, space small plants 30–36 in (75–90 cm) apart in a well-prepared trench. When planting, always remember that a hedge 6 ft (1.8 m) high may be 40–60 in (1–1.5 m) thick at its base. Trim it carefully during the first few years — you should really only cut back side shoots that have grown away from the line of the hedge. Later, you can start to shape the hedge so it is wider at the base than at the top. Finally the lead shoots should be cut about 1 ft (30 cm) below the intended ultimate height of the hedge. You should only need to trim a formal conifer hedge once a year. This is best done in June, so that the cut ends can heal before the winter.

You can also use conifers to make a less formal hedge, which retains the shapes of the individual trees. Choose smaller-growing subjects for

A formal hedge

Erica terminalis 'Thelma Woolner' used as a hedge

this type of hedge. The plant spacing will depend on the growth habit of the cultivars you have chosen, and will be wider than the spacing for a formal hedge.

Shrub heathers make excellent decorative hedges. Among the best plants for this purpose are *Erica terminalis* (either the species or the cultivar 'Thelma Woolner') and *E. erigena* 'Alba' or 'Superba'.

In the southern half of the UK the species *Erica terminalis* can reach 8 ft (2.5 m) or more. 'Thelma Woolner' can be kept at about half that height, but may be smaller in the north. Both of them are covered with cerise-pink flowers from July to November, and bees seem to be very fond of them!

Erica erigena 'Alba' and 'Superba' can reach 6 ft 6 in (2 m) or more, while cultivars such as 'Brightness' and 'W. T. Rackliff' are about half that height. Their main flush of bloom is from March until May, but they may produce a few flowers at any time from November onwards. They can be rather tender in exposed areas, and sub-zero winds can cut them to the ground. But if this does happen they usually show signs of recovery before the longest day. Cut them back to about 8 in (20 cm) above the ground to encourage the new growth to fill in.

You can either leave heather hedges to their own devices, or trim them to keep them in order. Trim them lightly, and

only in the green wood. Don't cut back into the wood towards the centre, which has lost its leaves. *Erica terminalis* should be trimmed in mid-March. However, you can trim *E. erigena* cultivars as soon as they have finished flowering, since this species blooms on the previous year's growth.

Rock gardens

Many books suggest growing conifers and heathers in rock gardens, and they can look superb in such a setting. When you see a natural rock garden in the wild, the effect can be stunning. However, building a rock garden is an expensive

Heather grows on rocks in the wild, making it a natural choice for a rock garden. But creating such a garden is not as easy as it may seem.

business, and many of the 'rockeries' that you see in gardens are disappointing. To ensure success, you must set large pieces of matching rock into the soil in such a way that they seem to be following natural strata. Then you can position plants in suitable pockets of soil between the rocks. A few large rocks can often be more effective than many small ones.

An alternative to a rock garden is a scree bed, where conifers and heathers are grown through small stones or gravel. This can be combined with one or more large rocks.

Topiary

So far, with the exception of formal hedges, we've been looking at conifers in their natural form. However, gardeners have been training conifers into fantastic shapes for many centuries. These can be simple geometric designs, arches or animals — real or imaginary. They're usually set in gravel or grass, but you can grow them in large pots or containers. The yew (*Taxus*

baccata) is the only conifer suitable for topiary.

Topiary is an art form, and this book is not the place for a discussion of its finer points. If you would like to explore the subject of topiary in more depth, then you should consult a more specialist volume on the subject.

In this knot garden Erica erigena 'W. T. Rackliff' and 'Golden Lady' create the framework, with E. e. 'Irish Dusk' as the dot plants, and Calluna vulgaris 'Clare Carpet' as the ground cover.

Knot gardens

Knot gardens are an old system of gardening based on clipped box hedges. They can be attractive, and seem to be coming back into fashion.

The compact and slow-growing cultivars of *Erica erigena* are ideal for this purpose. The contrasting foliage colours can be stunning, and the flowers are a welcome bonus.

In containers

Window boxes and tubs are ideal places to display dwarf and slower-growing plants of both heathers and conifers. You may need to move the heathers after a couple of years' growth.

The dwarf and slow-growing conifers are ideal for container gardening because the consequent restrictions placed on their roots will help to control their growth. Always bear in mind that container-grown plants will invariably need more attention, and take particular care about watering them in dry conditions.

Hanging baskets are not generally suitable for displaying conifers and heathers. However, some of the more trailing *Erica carnea* cultivars will do well in a winter basket provided you keep them well watered.

Heathers in a tub make a glorious display, but you should always bear in mind that they need a lot of care and attention.

Bonsai

You will sometimes see very beautiful examples of this Japanese art of artificially dwarfing trees. Many of the specimens are conifers. You can also practise it on the taller-growing heathers, though this is much less common.

You can't help admiring the artistic and horticultural skills of those who have produced these miniature masterpieces, but when you look at them you have the uneasy feeling that they've been somehow mutilated. If you're interested in growing bonsai for yourself, there are plenty of books on bonsai techniques, and a general introduction in the current *Step-by-step Gardening Guides* series.

Cultural requirements

We've already looked at the differences between conifers and heathers. They are very different plants, originating in very different parts of the world, so it's hardly surprising that they should have very different cultural requirements. You may see heathers growing at the edges of conifer plantations. You may even see the occasional pine or juniper standing in lonely isolation on a heather moor. But in nature, these plants do not grow together in the way that some gardeners choose to arrange them. You must understand what the plants themselves need if you want to grow them successfully.

Soil

Soils can be classified according to their physical structure. They may be light and sandy, medium and loamy, heavier or lighter clays, or intermediate between these types.

The chemical character of the soil may depend on the rocks from which it was formed, or on the way in which vegetation has decayed on it. It may, for instance, be acid or alkaline. The degree of acidity or alkalinity is expressed in pH values. A pH value of between

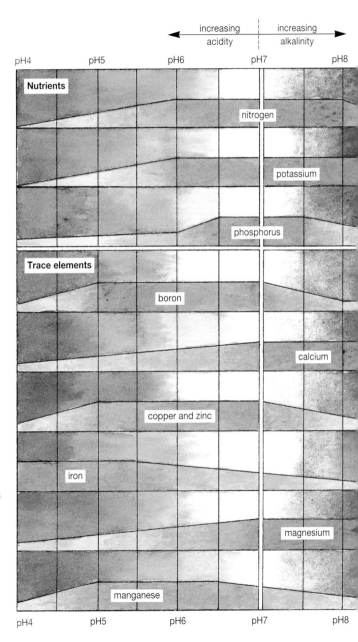

The relationship between the pH of the soil and the availability of nutrients and trace elements

14

0 and 7 indicates an acid soil, and the degree of acidity falls as the pH value rises. Between pH values 7 and 14 the soil is alkaline, and the degree of alkalinity increases with the pH value. Strictly speaking, pH 7 is neither acid nor alkaline, and soils with a pH close to 7 are said to be neutral.

As a general rule, conifers aren't particularly demanding as regards the soil in which they grow. However, they do prefer deep, moist, loamy soils. Few are happy growing on thin, chalky soils, and if that is your problem it's best to stick to juniper (*Juniperus*) and yew (*Taxus*) species. This is not a serious drawback, as these two genera provide a wide range of sizes, habits and foliage colours. On the other hand, there are a number of genera and species that won't thrive in anything but an acid soil. The table overleaf lists those lime-hating conifers that will not tolerate an alkaline soil.

Measuring the pH of the soil

The pH of the soil affects the nutrients and trace elements available to the plants. Acid-loving conifers and heathers are specially adapted to living in low-nitrogen environments. Symbiotic fungi called *mycorrhizae* live in their roots, and help to extract nutrients from poor soils.

Clearly, you need to know whether your soil is acid or alkaline before you decide what to grow. The presence of certain plants can give an indication. If rhododendrons or wild heather are growing, this is a clear sign of acidity, while beech (*Fagus sylvatica*) or yew (*Taxus baccata*) suggest that the soil may be alkaline. If you're in any doubt, you can test the soil.

You can buy soil test kits at garden centres for a few pounds (or even a few pence). The simplest include a single test (using a graduated tube for the test powder),

a colour chart, and instructions for use. More sophisticated kits will provide a tube of test tablets that allow a number of tests to be made.

The method of testing is the same in both cases. Take a sample of soil from several inches below the surface, and remove any stones or pieces of vegetable matter. Dry the soil and crumble it into the small test tube, up to the level indicated in your instructions. Add a test tablet and a set amount of distilled water, again as instructed. Then shake the tube thoroughly and put it to one side, giving time for the soil to settle and the colour to develop in the clear solution above it. You can then match it to a colour on the chart included with your pack. Each colour represents a known level of acidity or alkalinity.

It's a good idea to make several tests in the area where you intend to plant.

This will show up any variations or anomalies. If the ground has been cultivated in the past, then previous owners may have limed all or part of it to create an alkaline pocket in an acid area.

You may come across some cheap electronic devices claiming to be soil pH meters. They consist of a metal probe attached to a meter, which apparently gives a direct reading of pH levels. Unfortunately, however, most of these meters measure resistivity, not pH. The technicalities are a little complex, but the important thing is that these two soil characteristics are not directly related. If you want to use one of these meters, then calibrate it first by checking it with a number of solutions that have a known pH.

Lime-hating conifers

Abies amabilis
A. balsamea
A. firma
A. magnifica
A. mariesii
A. procera
A. veitchii

Chamaecyparis pisifera
C. thyoides

Larix

Picea engelmannii

Pinus densiflora
P. echinata
P. elliotii
P. lelophylla
P. luchuensis
P. monticola
P. patula
P. peuce

Pinus pseudostrobus
P. pumila
P. pungens
P. radiata
P. resinosa
P. rigida
P. × schwerinii
P. strobus
P. virginiana
P. washoensis

Podocarpus macrophyllus

Pseudolarix

Pseudotsuga

Sciadopitys

Taxodium

Tsuga caroliniana
T. diversifolia
T. heterophylla

Heathers need light, free-draining soils — they won't tolerate heavy clays. If your soil is a heavy clay, you will need to lighten it before planting out heathers.

All heather species will grow in acid soil, but some will tolerate neutral or even alkaline soils. It is therefore quite important to know the pH of your soil before selecting heather plants.

Soil requirements of heathers

Acid	Neutral	Alkaline
Andromeda latifolia	Daboecia cantabrica	Erica carnea
A. polifolia	Erica arborea (with	E. × darleyensis
Bruckenthalia spiculifolia	sufficient magnesium)	E. erigena
Calluna vulgaris	E. scoparia	E. lusitanica
Erica australis	E. vagans (with sufficient	E. manipuliflora
E. ciliaris	magnesium)	E. manipuliflora × E. vagans
E. cinerea	E. × williamsii	E. multiflora
E. mackaiana		E. × oldenburgensis
E. × stuartii		E. terminalis
E. tetralix		E. × veitchii
E. umbellata		
E. × watsonii		

Above *An exposed garden in winter, when some upright conifers are liable to suffer from wind burn.*

Right *Heathers do best in a sunny site that also receives plenty of rain.*

Positioning

Conifers may be planted either in full sun or in damp shade. But some will tolerate shade better than others. Cultivars of *Chamaecyparis obtusa, C. pisifera, Cephalotaxus, Cryptomeria japonica, Juniperus × media, J. sabina, J. squamata* and *Taxus baccata* are particularly suitable. Their ability to tolerate shade makes some of them invaluable for ground cover in some situations.

An excessively cold, windy site may prove unsuitable for some of the upright conifers. They may suffer *wind burn*, which causes the foliage to die on one side of the tree. A more important consideration is the dryness of certain parts of the garden. Conifers take water in through their roots and also their foliage. In the UK most rain is carried on winds from the southwest, so there are usually dry areas on the eastern and northeastern sides of your house (or of any high wall or fence). When you're watering the garden in hot, dry weather, don't forget to spray the foliage of your conifers.

To some extent the right place for a conifer depends on the way you want to use it. If you're planting shelter belts, for example, they should stand on the windward side of the area you want to protect. Plants for hedging must be set where the hedge is required.

The roots of conifers can directly affect and damage buildings, walls and underground services. Some large conifers produce a mat of roots close to the soil surface.

These will take a lot of water, and may kill grass or other plants in the vicinity. Others may take large amounts of water from the subsoil, which can have an adverse effect on buildings in clay areas. For guidance on planting trees next to buildings look in British Standard BS5837: 1991, *Guide for Trees in relation to construction* or *National House Builders Council Standards*, Chapter 4.2. You can obtain copies from your local public library.

In general, heathers should be planted in full sun. In the wild, most species grow in open spaces on heaths, moorland, bog and mountainsides. Some species come from the Mediterranean region and prefer full sun under British conditions. Heathers planted in dry, shady conditions will never thrive. The ideal aspect is facing south or southwest (for sun and rain).

There are three very good reasons for planting heathers well away from trees. Firstly, mature trees will take a great deal of moisture from the ground, which will make it too dry for the heathers. Secondly, the shade cast by trees will severely reduce the amount of flower, and prevent the development of good foliage colour. Thirdly, the falling leaves in the autumn must be cleared from the heathers. If they're allowed to rot on the plants they will smother and kill them.

Most heathers will tolerate a windy site, even at the seaside, though some of the more tender species do need protection from east and northeast winds in winter.

Other factors

It is extremely important to consider the final size of any conifer before you plant it. You must be sure that it will have enough space when it grows.

Some conifers are slow to establish themselves, and appear to 'stand still' in the garden for about five years. After that they will grow very quickly, and may well take up far more space than you had intended to give them. Don't forget that conifers planted in front of windows may grow big enough to obscure views and rob rooms of light. Some of the prostrate and semi-prostrate junipers will need constant pruning to control their size and spread. You may have to choose between sacrificing the surrounding plants and removing the offending conifer. Sometimes removal is the only practical course of action.

At the other end of the scale, choosing small and slow-growing conifers can be more

This conifer has been overgrown by the heathers planted around it.

18

Choosing plants

Know the pH of the soil

The first consideration has to be the pH of your soil. With alkaline soil, choosing the right plants is an absolute must if you want to avoid disappoint-

*Both this winter display (**left**) and the summer display (**below**) have been grown on alkaline soil.*

ment. Some conifers need acid soil, as do many heathers. But it is perfectly possible to grow conifers and heathers on an alkaline soil, as these two pictures demonstrate.

For alkaline soils on chalk or limestone, with a pH of 7 or more, you'll need lime-tolerant plants. As far as conifers are

difficult if you intend to plant heathers around them. The shapes, colours and textures of the dwarf conifers are very attractive, and a surrounding group of heathers will set them off very well. You'll obviously need to choose low-growing heathers for this purpose. Some cultivars of *Calluna vulgaris* or *Erica carnea* will grow no taller than 6 in (15 cm), which ensures they will not swamp the conifers.

Many people have the mistaken idea that heathers can withstand drought. This is certainly not the case. They should be watered regularly in dry weather between March and October. Don't feed them, however, except on the poorest sandy soils — though it's a good idea to mulch them with peat, leafmould or bark chippings. This should be done when the soil is properly wet.

Well-grown conifers in large containers are more difficult to establish.

concerned, it's best to stick to junipers (*Juniperus*) and yews (*Taxus baccata*) on very thin chalky soils. On deeper alkaline loams, *Chamaecyparis lawsoniana* and *Thuja* species will succeed. The heathers will be mainly winter- and spring-flowering, with a few summer-flowering species to add colour between May and November. From November to May you can't beat the winter display of heathers in bloom, and their foliage will continue to provide colour all through the rest of the year.

On neutral soils (pH 6.5) you'll have a wider choice of heather species. Any heather can be grown on acid soil (pH 4.5-6.0), which will enable you to have flowers throughout the year. As long as there's enough sun to develop the foliage colour (and plenty of bloom), the choice is yours.

Selecting good-quality plants

Good-quality plants are essential. Conifers are on sale nowadays in a good range of pot sizes from rooted cuttings (liners) to well-grown plants in large containers. Obviously the larger plants are expensive, as are plants produced by grafting; most have been grown on with care and are of good quality, but they may be more difficult to establish than smaller plants. Whatever size you

choose, the foliage should be healthy, with no brown or dead patches. The root ball should be moist and weed-free. And there shouldn't be too many roots growing out of the pot.

When buying heathers, choose compact, bushy plants in preference to straggly, overgrown ones with open centres. A well-grown heather should have been trimmed regularly at the young stage to promote new growth from the centre of the plant. The root ball should be moist and weed-free, with no roots growing through the bottom of the pot. A heather that shows any sign of withering is dead. No amount of watering will revive it.

Younger plants tend to establish themselves quickly, and will soon make up the growth of the larger plants. Naturally, the larger plants will give a

more instant effect, and will cover the ground a year earlier than the smaller plants.

Garden centres offer a reasonable selection of both conifers and heathers. However, these establishments are geared to impulse buying. Heathers are usually offered only when in bloom, and some species are seldom seen.

For the more unusual plants it's worth seeking out specialist growers. You can find both plants and growers in *The RHS Plant Finder*, which is published annually. The 1997-98 edition lists 70,000 plants, and tells you where you can buy them. It gives the names, addresses and telephone numbers of the growers, together with their opening times, the price of their catalogues, and whether they will supply by mail order.

Planting

Preparation

It's vital to prepare the soil thoroughly before planting. Both heathers and conifers are long-lived. Heathers can be expected to provide colour, interest and ground cover for 10 to 25 years, while most conifers can have a considerably longer useful life. So it's worth the time and expense involved in preparing the ground properly.

In the earlier section on soil, we touched briefly on how to deal with heavy clays, but for planting it's helpful to know a little more about improving soil structure. There are a few simple rules that are worth following.

If your soil is light and free-draining, but sandy or stony, add plenty of humus (organic material) to improve moisture retention. Ideally this should be your own garden compost, as long as it isn't alkaline (if it is, follow the advice on mushroom compost given below). Alternatives are very well-rotted or composted manure, leaf-mould, moss peat or a peat substitute.

On chalky (alkaline) soils, where you're restricted to lime-tolerant species, you could use spent mushroom compost, which contains lime.

If you're going to plant heathers, then you must

lighten heavy clay soils. You can do this by adding coarse grit and humus and working it in to a depth of about 1 ft (30 cm). However, it's better to build up heather beds by producing a suitable mixture above the level of the existing clay. This prevents waterlogging and allows the soil to warm up quickly.

A new planting of heathers — to be sure of success, you should prepare the soil properly beforehand.

Planting through gravel

If you need to keep maintenance on the planting area to a minimum, then a good solution is to plant through a protective layer of gravel spread on polymer sheeting. If you choose this method, it's probably better to space the plants more widely.

Once you've finished your preparations, the ideal material for covering the ground is Plantex Mulch Mat® or a similar woven polypropylene. You can buy this at most garden centres. Water can easily penetrate this material, while weeds germinating underneath it cannot! It's also an effective smotherer of persistent weeds such as

Planting heather through gravel isn't difficult, and does away with the need for weeding.

ground elder (*Aegopodium podagraria*). The material must be laid, like a carpet, over the whole area, overlapping where necessary — it's important not to leave any gaps. When you've finished, cover it with a 2-3-inch (5-8 cm) layer of 6-9-mm lime-free gravel.

Planting isn't difficult. Just lay out the plants in the normal way, but on top of the gravel. Once you're satisfied with the arrangement, put in the individual plants as follows. Scrape back the gravel to reveal an area of polypropylene the size of a normal planting hole. Cut a cross in the matting and tuck it under itself. Dig a planting hole in the soil, and insert the

plant to a depth where its lower foliage will touch the gravel once it has been pushed back. Replace cut sections of polypropylene sheeting, and then push back the displaced gravel, carefully packing it under the foliage.

This style of planting can look very attractive. It will do away with the work of weeding while the plants are maturing, and reduce the amount of water that they need — but do water the plants well after you've put them in, and don't set them in very dry ground.

A variation of this technique was recently used at the Hilliers Arboretum at Romsey when the heather garden was

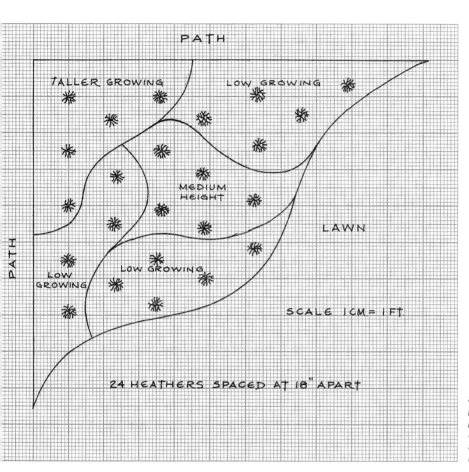

PATH

TALLER GROWING   LOW GROWING

MEDIUM
HEIGHT

LAWN

LOW
GROWING   LOW GROWING

PATH

SCALE I CM = I FT

24 HEATHERS SPACED AT 18" APART

A typical planting plan showing spacing for heathers

being restored. The gravel was replaced with a much thicker layer of composted bark. A Leaky Hose® irrigation system was positioned in the beds before the bark was laid down.

Spacing

It's good practice to prepare scale plans of your proposed planting on suitable squared paper (as in the figure above). This will help enormously when you're choosing and positioning cultivars.

Remember that it's vital to choose conifers for their size and for the space that you have available. Heathers are easier to deal with, as the spread of the plants is not so variable. Most plants are described as compact, medium-spreading or vigorous. Ground-cover plants will spread to a diameter of 18-24 in (45-60 cm) in three to four years. If you aim to achieve total ground cover in three to four years, then a good average planting distance is 18 in (45 cm) apart, i.e. four plants per sq yd/m². The more vigorous cultivars may, of course, be planted further apart, i.e. 2 ft or 2 ft 6 in (60-75 cm). It's a pity to over-plant with heathers and then find, two years or so later, that you have to move some of them.

23

Once you've decided on a layout for your planting, it's a good idea to put the pots on the ground in their correct places before you start to plant — this is particularly important when space is limited. Only start planting when you're satisfied that the layout is just as you want it.

If there's grass at the edge of your planting area, be sure to keep your plants away from the edge. That way, you can prevent them being cropped by the lawnmower when they mature. If there's paving at the edge, you might want to position your plants so that they spread over the edge and soften it. If you're planting against a wall, make sure the plants have enough space to spread towards the wall. And don't forget that a south- or west-facing wall is likely to reflect heat. In summer the temperature can rise significantly, and this will tend to draw moisture away from the bed. You must water enough to be sure that the plants nearest the wall don't dry out.

Planting holes for conifers and heathers must be deep enough to cover the root ball of the plant completely. They should also be considerably wider than the pot in which the plant is growing. The soil in the hole should have peat or some other organic matter well worked in, as should the soil you intend to use for back filling. For conifers you can sprinkle a little bonemeal into the hole.

Check the lower trunks of conifers for the tell-tale callus that shows they have been grafted. The callus should never be buried below the surface when you're planting. Non-grafted conifers should be planted so that the soil level in the pot coincides with the soil surface in the garden. Heathers should be planted a little deeper than they were grown in the nursery — their lower foliage should be resting on the ground.

Make sure the root ball is thoroughly wet before you

Above *A new planting of heathers on a bank*

Left *The same planting two years later — another year or two and the bed will be covered.*

A group of conifers covered with hoar frost makes a very attractive picture.

begin planting — if necessary, soak your plants with water over the top of the pot until no more bubbles rise from the pot; then drain them.

Carefully remove the pot from the root ball. For conifers, gently tease out any roots that may be spiralling round the pot. Turn the plant in the direction you want it and spread the roots out in the planting hole, just as you would with plants that have been grown in open ground. If you think a supporting stake will be necessary, now is the time to put it in, while you can still see (and therefore avoid) the roots.

Some heather plants may be very 'pot-bound' with an almost solid tangle of roots. If yours are like this, then tear the roots into four at the bottom before spreading them out in the planting hole.

Now refill your planting holes progressively with prepared soil, firming as you go. You need to remember that upright conifers must be able to resist wind rock, and that all recent plantings may suffer frost heave — but don't over-firm very wet or heavy soils. Finally, loosen the surface layer and water thoroughly.

In theory, container-grown plants may be planted at any time of year, as long as the ground isn't bone dry, water-logged or frozen solid. Even so, it's not a good idea to plant in the middle of a dry spell. No plant will get a good start in these conditions.

The autumn months (between mid-September and Christmas) are probably the best time for planting your conifers and heathers. The soil is usually well moistened by regular rainfall, and will still be warm. Planting in the autumn ensures that the plants will settle in well during the winter, and can cope with the drier conditions in the late spring and summer. After hard

This small heather bed has been planted with cultivars of Daboecia cantabrica, Erica erigena *and* E. carnea.

frosts, check for any plants that may have been lifted. You can re-firm them when the ground has completely thawed and is not too wet.

Young plants in their first year will need thorough watering. It's worth noting that some parts of the UK have had very dry springs from March onwards, as well as hot, dry summers. In the first year or two after planting, there will also be bare ground between the young plants, and this can

very easily dry out. As the plants mature and grow together, they will cover this bare ground; evaporation will reduce, and you won't need to water so often (though you will still need to do it).

At this point it's worth thinking about grouping plants together for maximum effect (though this topic is dealt with in more detail in the section on design ideas). Conifers grouped together in a planting can add a great deal of interest. Ideally, you should try to group one each of three or more different cultivars, and at the same time try to exploit variations in shape, height and colour. A group like this will

make an attractive backdrop for a heather planting. In general, heathers are more effective if they are planted in groups of no fewer than three per cultivar. You could plant a small area of 3 sq yd (2.5 m^2) with 12 plants, using three specimens of each of four different cultivars. Planting odd-numbered groups like this seems to work better — it avoids the appearance of regimented straight lines.

This specimen of Juniperus communis 'Compressa' *has been planted in a bed of* Erica carnea.

Maintenance

Weed control

You'll need to weed newly planted areas by hand at regular intervals. Always take particular care to remove any weed seedlings from under the plants, before they become established and overwhelm their host. If you were careful about preparing the ground before planting, there won't be many seeds left in the soil to germinate. However, during the spring and summer seeds are blown into gardens from trees, wild flowers and grasses.

Use a trowel, or even a hoe, to remove any seedlings that resist your efforts to pull them out — but if you do need a hoe, take great care not to damage the spreading roots of new plants.

The herbicide Casseron G has been successfully used to control weeds in the National Collection of *Calluna vulgaris* at the Northern Horticultural Society's gardens at Harlow Carr, Harrogate. This material must be used in accordance with the manufacturers' instructions. Don't allow it to come into contact with the heathers, and don't use it on a bed until the plants are fully established, roughly a year after planting.

Mulches

Using mulches has a number of advantages, and they will save time and energy once they're in place. They reduce the amount of weeding you have to do, and they conserve soil moisture, which reduces the need for watering. This last point is worth thinking about if your water supply is metered.

Mulches are layers of organic material spread between and under plants. They should be at least 1-2 in (2.5-5 cm) thick. If you wish, you can mulch new plants while planting them out, as long as you have soaked the soil thoroughly first. Depending on the type and amount of material you have used, you may need to renew mulches from time to time. This is best done in the early spring, before the winter rains have had a chance to evaporate.

You can buy chipped bark in various grades from fine chippings to coarse lumps. The coarse grades are ideal for trees, such as a specimen conifer planted in grass. Fine bark is useful in beds, around dwarf conifers and heathers. As well as having real advantages, mulches can be very attractive. However, newly chipped bark can look very stark and light, and can lock up available nitrogen as it breaks down. To minimise this drawback, and to improve the appearance of the mulch, you should buy it some time before you actually need it, and pile it somewhere to compost before you apply it.

Peat or a peat substitute may be preferable for mulching beds. You can use either moss or sedge peat. The advantage of peat is that it's absorbed into the soil more rapidly than bark, and this in turn improves the soil structure. Peat doesn't lock up nitrogen, and it also increases soil acidity.

If you want to mulch a bed permanently, you can plant heathers and conifers through plastic sheeting under a layer of gravel (see pages 21-2).

One major advantage of mulching is that it prevents evaporation — but it can also prevent water from reaching the roots of your plants. *Never* apply mulches to dry ground, and be sure to use plenty of water on mulched beds.

Watering

The importance of watering conifers and heathers cannot be stressed enough. These plants are not drought-resistant, and are exposed to high rainfall and misty conditions in their natural habitats

A few heather species from the Mediterranean region are accustomed to higher temperatures, but many of them grow close to water in the wild. So it's best to assume that *all* heathers need water.

Heathers and conifers, not forgetting the taller species, will always benefit if you spray water over their foliage as well as applying it to their roots.

Feeding

Most conifers and heathers grow naturally on impoverished soils. Young plants in nurseries are usually fed because they are grown in soilless composts. Once you've planted them, feeding is not really necessary. On the contrary, it can produce leggy, unnaturally vigorous growth.

The only exception is where plants are being grown on thin, sandy soils. Even here you should apply fertilisers only when there is a clear need for them — and you should always use them sparingly. It's vital for the plants to develop and grow in a natural way, retaining their compact habit.

Pruning

Many conifers need no pruning at all. These are the upright cone-shaped or dome-shaped dwarf types. It's also better not to prune the larger trees, unless disease makes it necessary or they outgrow the space available for them. In either case this is probably work for a qualified tree surgeon, who should also be employed if you want to remove a large tree.

The prostrate and semi-prostrate conifers may need some pruning when they are young — this will encourage them to thicken from the centre. You can cut back the lead branches by one-third of their length at

any time between June and September. June is preferable, though, as it will give time for the plants to grow over the cut branches during the following three months. As the plant matures, you may also want to prune lightly to keep it thick and bushy. You can reduce the spread of a prostrate or semi-prostrate cultivar by trimming back the lower branches. This allows the shorter, higher branches to droop down and hide the cuts. Again, June is the best month for either of these tasks.

Tall conifers used for hedging or screening will thicken if you prune them lightly while they are maturing. This will also create denser growth. Once formal hedges are established, they will obviously need an annual clipping to keep them neat and tidy.

The pruning of heathers has always been rather controversial. But the lower-growing species — i.e. those growing up to about 40 in (1 m) — will

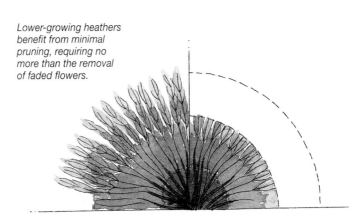

Lower-growing heathers benefit from minimal pruning, requiring no more than the removal of faded flowers.

most likely benefit from an annual pruning. Remove faded flowers, but don't reveal the bare wood at the heart of the plant. If plants have bloomed between June and November, then you're recommended to trim them in mid-March, once the worst of the winter weather has passed. In northern parts of the UK you may need to wait another couple of weeks. You can trim as soon as new growth starts to appear.

Plants that flower between late November and early May should be trimmed as soon as they finish flowering. With late bloomers you may find it necessary to remove the flowers. New growth will be visible from mid-March, and you'll undoubtedly need to remove some of it during pruning. Don't worry: it will renew itself in time to produce flower buds in June and July, ready for the following winter and spring.

If you trim these lower-growing species every year, they will develop into very bushy, well-clothed plants. They will last much longer than untrimmed plants, and will tend to smother any neighbouring weeds.

One exceptional group of heathers consists of the tree heaths *Erica arborea*, *E. lusitanica*, their hybrid *E. × veitchii* and their cultivars. These should be cut back by one-third for the first three or four years. This will ensure that they remain well covered with foliage right down to the

Exceptional among the heathers are some of the tree heaths — Erica arborea, E. lusitanica, their hybrid E. × veitchii and their cultivars — which should be cut back by one-third for the first three or four years.

ground. It will also stop them developing multiple bare, straggly trunks. Pruning is best done in late May.

The remaining taller heathers — *Erica australis*, *E. erigena* and *E. terminalis* — may benefit from light trimming, which encourages the plants to thicken up. *E. australis* and *E. erigena* cultivars can be trimmed immediately after flowering, but don't trim *E. terminalis* until March. After the first few years it's up to you — you can either trim the plants to maintain a neat, formal appearance, or leave them to grow naturally.

Conifer genera, species and cultivars

The 800 or so species of conifer have provided the subject for several learned tomes, and *The RHS Plant Finder 1997-98* lists over 1,650 species and cultivars of conifers.

Obviously, in the limited space available here, we can provide only the briefest of glimpses into the world of conifers, so regrettably a lot has had to be left out.

A word of warning
The names of conifers often seem forbidding. Even so, it's well worth trying to master them. If you study any list of conifers, you'll notice that the same species names are used in different genera. You'll also notice that many cultivar names, especially the older ones in Latin form, are used in several species.

The different shapes of conifer

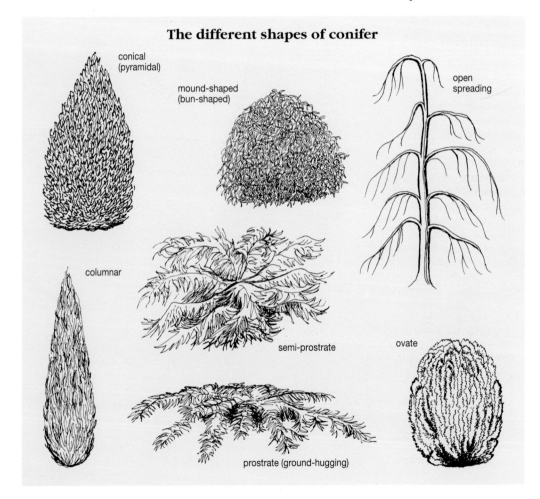

conical (pyramidal)

mound-shaped (bun-shaped)

open spreading

columnar

semi-prostrate

ovate

prostrate (ground-hugging)

To identify accurately which plant you are talking about you *must* have the right **genus**, **species** and **cultivar name** (see the panel on page 6). This will also ensure that you get the plant you really want at the nursery or garden centre.

Abies (Pinaceae) Silver firs

This is a genus of around 60 species. The names of some of them demonstrate its wide distribution in the Northern Hemisphere, where it reaches as far south as Taiwan and Central America. Towards the southern end of its range it is restricted to mountains.

Abies is distinguished from *Picea* by the cones, which grow upwards from the tops of the branches. They don't fall — they simply disintegrate on the branches when they are ripe. The circular leaf scars are another distinguishing feature.

Of the 60 or so species, about 28 are available in the UK, and 19 have produced cultivars. The species are characterised by large conical trees, growing

Some species of *Abies*

A. alba (European silver fir)
A. amabilis, (red silver fir)
A. arizonica
A. balsamea (balsam fir)
A. borisii-regis
A. bornmuelleriana
A. bracteata (Santa Lucia fir)
A. cephalonica (Greek fir)
A. chengii
A. chensiensis
A. cilicia (Cilician fir)
A. concolor (Colorado white fir)
A. delavayi
A. fabri
A. fargesii
A. firma (Japanese fir)
A. fraseri
A. gamblie
A. georgei
A. grandis (giant fir)
A. holophylla (Manchurian fir)
A. homolepis (Nikko fir)
A. kawakamii
A. koreana

A. lasiocarpa (subalpine fir)
A. magnifica (Californian red fir)
A. mariesii (Maries fir)
A. nebrodensis
A. nordmanniana (Caucasian fir)
A. numidica (Algerian fir)
A. oaxacana
A. pindrow (West Himalayan fir)
A. pinsapo (Spanish fir)
A. procera (noble fir)
A. recurvata
A. religiosa (sacred fir)
A. sachalinensis (Sachalin fir)
A. spectabilis (Himalayan fir)
A. squamata (Flakey fir)
A. × vasconellosiana (*A. pindrow × A. pinsapo*)
A. veitchii (Veitch's silver fir)
A. vejari
A. × vilmorinii (*A. cephalonica × A. pinsapo*)

as high as 200 ft (60m) in their native habitats. They are generally rather smaller in cultiva-tion, but still only suitable for planting as specimens in very large gardens.

Most of us will probably be more interested in the dwarf and slow-growing cultivars. One of the most popular of these is *A. balsamea* **f. hudsonia**. It forms a small, compact dome, which may grow to 30 in (75 cm) tall, with a spread of about 5 ft (1.5 m), in 30 years. It has dark-green leaves that are borne semi-radially, leaving a 'parting' along the stem. This helps to

Species and cultivars of *Abies* that have received an Award of Garden Merit (AGM) from the Royal Horticultural Society (RHS)

A. balsamea f. *hudsonia*
A. concolor
A. concolor 'Compacta'
A. grandis
A. koreana 'Silberlocke'
A. lasiocarpa 'Arizonica Compacta'

A. nordmanniana
A. nordmanniana 'Golden Spreader'
A. pinsapo 'Glauca'
A. procera
A. veitchii

distinguish it from another dwarf cultivar *A. balsamea* 'Nana', which carries its needles radially and so lacks the parting. These cultivars are not fully lime-tolerant.

A. concolor 'Compacta' (*A. c.* var. *glauca* 'Compacta' or *A. c.* 'Glauca Compacta') is the only dwarf Colorado fir — a slow-growing shrub with an irregular habit. The grey-blue foliage is at its brightest from May to July. Various authorities give different estimates of its size, but it is unlikely to reach 3 ft (1 m) in ten years, and will only reach about 6 ft (1.8 m) in height and spread at full maturity. You may have to visit a specialist nursery to find it.

Abies koreana 'Silberlocke' (*A. k.* 'Horstmann's Silberlocke') was raised in Germany before 1983. It has a conical habit, similar to that of the species, but has been selected for its slower growth rate. The leaves curl upwards, revealing white undersides. This cultivar bears 2 in (5 cm) violet cones from an early age. It will probably grow to a maximum 10 ft (3 m) in ten years but can eventually grow to be more than 33 ft (10 m) tall.

A. lasiocarpa 'Arizonica Compacta' (*A. l.* var. *arizonica* 'Compacta', *A. l.* 'Compacta') is a slow-growing cultivar of the cork fir. This name refers to the bark, which is thick, soft, and corky — useful for conserving moisture in its native habitat. The cultivar has an irregular conical habit and grey-green leaves. It is said to have an ultimate height of 6 ft (1.8 m).

A. nordmanniana, the Caucasian fir, is another large, conical tree, clothed to the ground with layers of drooping branches. The foliage is dark glossy green, with reddish-brown winter buds. It normally grows to around 16 ft (5 m) in height after ten years, but its ultimate height may be 165–195 ft (50–60 m).

The species has produced a dwarf form called **'Golden Spreader'**. This cultivar has bright-golden foliage, and the colour intensifies in winter. In the summer it needs a little shade to protect it from scorching. It is reputed to grow to only 12 in (30 cm) high and 20 in (50 cm) across after ten years. A slightly larger cultivar is *A. n.* **'Barabits' Spreader'** ('Barabits' Gold') This has light-green branches with golden tips.

Left Abies lasiocarpa *'Arizonica Compacta'*

Abies nordmanniana *'Barabits' Gold'*

Cedrus deodar *'Aurea'*

Araucaria (Araucariaceae)

Most people will be familiar with the monkey puzzle tree or Chilean pine (*A. araucana*), with its formal outline and stiffly curving branches. It is the only representative of this family that is hardy in Britain. It was much planted by the Victorians and Edwardians, but seems to have fallen out of favour in recent times.

There are two antipodean species which are now being grown in warmer parts of the world. They are the bunya-bunya (*A. bidwilli*) from coastal Queensland, and the Norfolk Island pine (*A. hetero-phylla*). I have seen the Norfolk Island pine grown as an attractive pot plant in England. All three species make large trees and all have edible seeds.

Calocedrus (Cupressaceae)

Calocedrus is a small genus of three species, of which only *C. decurrens*, the incense cedar, is truly hardy in the UK. This tree originated in North America. It has a dense colum-nar habit. The branchlets are arranged in flattened sprays, and the scale-like leaves are dark green. In good growing conditions it can reach a height of 150 ft (45 m). It was award-ed an AGM in 1992.

There is an American cultivar, *C. decurrens* 'Intricata' ('Nana'), which was raised in

1938. It forms a dense, rigid column, with thick, flat, twist-ed recurving branches. Appar-ently it was 4 ft (1.2 m) tall by 2 ft (60 cm) in diameter after 20 years, and doubled those figures after another 20 years.

Species and cultivars of *Cedrus* that were awarded an AGM by the RHS in 1992

C. deodara
C. deodara 'Aurea'
C. libani brevifolia,
C. libani libani
C. libani var. *atlantica*
  Glauca Group
  (*C. atlantica* 'Glauca')

Cedrus (Pinaceae) Cedars

Some botanists would argue that there are four or possibly five species in this genus, which includes several popular species and cultivars.

C. deodara, the deodar or Himalayan cedar, was intro-duced into the UK in 1831. It is distinguished from the other cedars by its longer leaves, which can be up to 2 in (5 cm) long. It is a fast-growing tree, but seldom lives more than 100 years. It has a curving leader, and the tips of its spreading branches droop, which gives the tree a rather limp and pendulous habit. The foliage is dark green. At ten

This cedar of Lebanon (Cedrus libani libani) *has grown to full maturity.*

arranged rather like those of *Cedrus libani libani*, but it differs in having a narrowly conical habit. Its leaves are only 0.5 in (1-1.25 cm) long when mature. It may be no more than 40 in (1 m) tall after ten years, but since its introduction specimens have been known to reach a height of 70 ft (21 m) and a diameter of 5 ft (1.5 m).

C. libani libani, the cedar of Lebanon, was introduced into the UK as long ago as 1638. With its stout, curving trunk, flat open crown and dark green foliage it is a well-known sight in many parks, large gardens and churchyards. It can reach a height of 130 ft (40 m) with considerable girth

years old the deodar will normally be 10-16 ft (3-5 m) tall, but it can eventually grow as tall as 165 ft (50 m).

The gold-foliage cultivar *C. deodara* 'Aurea' (pictured on the previous page) shares the habit of the species, but is altogether less robust. Its

height after ten years is likely to be only 4-5 ft (1.2-1.5 m), while at maturity it is unlikely to exceed 16 ft (5 m).

C. libani brevifolia, the Cypress cedar, was introduced from the mountains of Cyprus in 1875. This is a very slow-growing tree, with its branches

and spread. Many of our finest specimens are now reaching full maturity, and it is certainly to be hoped that there are people with the foresight, and the opportunity, to plant more of them now for the benefit of future generations.

C. libani **'Golden Dwarf'** ('Prostrata Aurea') doesn't really live up to either of its names. It is sometimes prostrate, but is not suited to the smaller garden. For those who have the space, it does have pleasant golden foliage that becomes brighter in winter.

A number of slow-growing seedlings of *C. libani* have been selected and distributed under the cultivar name 'Nana'.

Right Cedrus libani *'Nana'*

Below Cedrus libani *'Golden Dwarf'* *('Prostrata Aurea')*

Plants offered as *C. libani* 'Nana' may therefore show greater variation than is found in a true clone, and they should now correctly be called *C. libani* Nana Group. However, all of them will grow slowly into medium-sized conical bushes.

C. libani **var. *atlantica* Glauca Group** (pictured overleaf) is, even now, more likely to be encountered under the name of *C. atlantica* 'Glauca'. Plants grown under this name come from one of many selections made from the Atlas cedar, which is found in the

35

Atlas Mountains of Algeria and Morocco. They grow into erect, conical trees with upward-sweeping branches clothed in grey or silver-blue foliage. With age, some of the lower branch-

A mature specimen of Cedrus atlantica *'Glauca'*

es may bend downwards, almost touching the ground.

C. atlantica 'Glauca' is among the most beautiful of all conifers, but is all too often planted in small or medium-sized gardens, where it can never reach its full majesty. After ten years it grows up to

10-13 ft (3-4 m) tall, with a branch spread of perhaps 6 ft 6 in (2 m). At maturity, it may well be 115-130 ft (35-40 m) tall, with branches spreading 65 ft (20 m).

Cephalotaxus (Cephalotaxaceae) Plum yews

This is a small genus of four species of shrubs, native to the Himalayas and eastern Asia. They tolerate shade, and grow well on alkaline (chalk and limestone) soils.

C. fortunei, the Chinese plum yew, makes a spreading bush with glossy dark-green leaves 2-3.5 in (6-9 cm) long. After ten years it will probably be 10 ft (3 m) tall and rather wider in spread. It derives its popular name from the shape of its olive-brown fruits, which appear only on female trees.

The cultivar *C. fortunei* **'Prostrate Spreader'** is well described by its name. It is an excellent ground-cover plant, especially valuable for its ability to thrive in shade on chalky soils. At maturity you can expect it to have a spread of 13 ft (4 m), though it will only be about 30 in (80 cm) tall.

The other species of garden interest is *C. harringtonia*. The cultivar 'Fastigiata' is like a large-leaved Irish yew. All the stems grow vertically, producing a narrow, columnar tree with dark-green foliage. It is a slow starter, and will probably be no more than 5 ft (1.5 m) tall after ten years. Ultimately it

Cephalotaxus harringtonia *var.* drupacea *'Duke Gardens'*

will grow to between 10 ft (3 m) and 13 ft (4 m).

C. harringtonia var. drupacea is known as the Japanese plum yew or cow's tail pine. It is a dense, spreading bush with drooping branchlets. In ten years it can reach a height of 6 ft 6 in (2 m). The ultimate height is about 10 ft (3 m), with a rather larger spread. It can tolerate colder conditions than its Chinese cousin.

Chamaecyparis (Cupressaceae) False cypresses

Chamaecyparis is a genus of seven species, native to North America, Japan and Taiwan.

The Greek prefix *Chamae-* indicates a dwarfing habit, but in this case only in relation to the true cypresses (*Cupressus*). False cypresses differ from *Cupressus* in their flattened, frond-like branchlets and smaller cones. The cones of *Chamaecyparis* develop, ripen

Chamaecyparis species

C. formosensis (Taiwan cypress)

C. henryae

C. lawsoniana (Lawson cypress)

C. nootkatensis (Nootka cypress)

C. obtusa (Hinoki cypress)

C. pisifera (Sawara cypress)

C. thyoides (white cypress)

Chamaecyparis cultivars that have received an Award of Garden Merit

C. lawsoniana
'Aurea Densa'
'Chilworth Silver'
'Ellwoodii'
'Ellwood's Gold'
'Fletcheri'
'Gimbornii'
'Grayswood Pillar'
'Green Hedger'
'Intertexta'
'Kilmacurragh'
'Lane'
'Lutea'
'Lutea Nana'
'Minima Aurea'
'Minima Glauca'
'Pelt's Blue'
'Pembury Blue'
'Pygmaea Argentea'
'Stardust'
'Wisselii'

C. nootkatensis
'Pendula'

C. obtusa
'Crippsii'
'Nana Aurea'
'Nana Gracilis'
'Tetragona Aurea'

C. pisifera
'Boulevard'
'Filifera Aurea'
'Golden Mop'

C. thyoides
'Andelyensis'
'Andelyensis Nana'
'Ericoides'

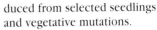

and shed their seed in a single year, while those of *Cupressus* require 18 months or more to mature, and even then don't shed their seed for a number of years.

Chamaecyparis grow well in moist, well-drained soils, but more slowly in chalky ones. They resent strong prevailing winds, especially if they are laden with salt.

Chamaecyparis lawsoniana
Lawson cypress

The tree is native to southwest Oregon and northwest California, where it is found between 4,000 ft (1,200 m) and 6,000 ft (1,800 m) above sea level. The first seeds were sent to Lawson's nursery in Edinburgh in 1854, and since then over 200 named cultivars have been pro-

duced from selected seedlings and vegetative mutations.

The species is a tall, narrowly conical tree with a drooping lead shoot. The foliage, which covers the plant almost to the ground, is dark green and scale-like. Specimens in Great Britain have been recorded at 130 ft (40 m) tall with a diameter of about 13 ft (4 m).

The cultivars show a wide range of growth habits, ranging from tall trees to slow-growing and even dwarf plants. Among them you can find foliage in every shade of green, grey, blue, and yellow. Some foliage is even variegated.

With so many cultivars available, it's hard to make a selection, so we have preferred to ignore those offered only by a few specialist growers. It also seemed wise to avoid recent introductions, since no one yet knows how they will perform as they mature.

We shall begin with a group of cultivars that make excellent 'lawn specimens'. They can also be used in background groups for larger gardens. **'Pembury Blue'**, **'Fraseri'** and **'Golden Wonder'** all grow to about 6–8 ft (2–2.5 m) tall after ten years, but in good growing conditions they can achieve between 33 ft (10 m) and 50 ft (15 m) at maturity.

Lawn specimens of Chamaecyparis lawsoniana, *showing (left) 'Pembury Blue' almost hiding 'Fraseri', (centre) 'Golden Wonder' and (right)* Thuja plicata *'Zebrina Extra Gold'*

'Ellwoodii' was introduced in 1929, and is quite well known. It forms a dense ovate tree with dark-green foliage growing almost to the ground. Mature specimens have a short, stout trunk, but divide into a number of vertical branches. As a result, the tree can occasionally open up under heavy snowfalls.

The cultivars 'Alumii' (1890) and 'Fletcheri' (1913; AGM in 1984 and 1993) both have blue-grey foliage. The former has the single, drooping lead shoot of the species, while the latter is multi-stemmed. Both have been overtaken in popularity by the more recently introduced 'Pembury Blue' (see previous page) with its brighter foliage, which forms a rather open, multi-stemmed tree. To these may be added 'Grayswood Pillar', a very narrow columnar tree with blue-green foliage. 'Green Pillar' has a broader columnar habit, and like 'Pottenii' it has bright-green foliage.

'Golden Wonder' has yellow foliage. 'Lane', sometimes known as 'Lanei', 'Lutea' or 'Stewartii', is an alternative yellow-foliage cultivar that eventually makes a large tree.

Turning to trees of more modest stature, it may be as well to regard them as slow-growing rather than dwarfs. 'Ellwood's Gold', a sport from 'Ellwoodii' (see above), is not a true gold-leaved plant but has yellow tips to its green foliage. It is much slower-growing than its dark-green progenitor. It should reach a height of about 6–8 ft (2–2.5 m) in ten years, and can grow between 10 ft (3 m) and 13 ft (4 m) in height at maturity. 'Blom' is a blue, upright-growing cultivar that is suitable for the smaller garden. The foliage is arranged in a vertical plane. At ten years old it should be about 6 ft 6 in (2 m) tall and 16 in (40 cm) wide. 'Treasure' is another small, columnar tree with variegated foliage.

Chamaecyparis lawsoniana
'Treasure'

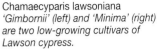

Chamaecyparis lawsoniana *'Gimbornii' (left) and 'Minima' (right) are two low-growing cultivars of Lawson cypress.*

globe of dark, bluish-green foliage, while **'Green Globe'** is if anything even smaller, growing to around 12 in (30 cm) tall after ten years.

Also of interest is **'Pygmy Argentea'** ('Backhouse Silver'), which was raised by James Backhouse and Sons of York in the late 19th century. It is very slow-growing, reaching 8–12 in (20–30 cm) in ten years and only 40 in (1 m) at maturity. The foliage is dark green with silver-grey edges to each whorl, though the plant must be grown in full sun to develop this character to the full. Frost or cold winds may cause it temporary damage. **'Nana Argentea'** is a very similar cultivar.

There are other cultivars that form ball-like plants. **'Aurea Densa'** arose as a seedling almost 90 years ago. It slowly forms a dense, upright-growing bush with golden-yellow foliage. A mature specimen may be no more than 4 ft (1.2 m) tall by 40 in (1 m) wide after 30 or 40 years. **'Minima Aurea'** is a similar plant.

'Minima' and **'Nana'** are similar in size and habit to those already mentioned, but they both have green foliage. **'Gimbornii'** makes a neat

Below right Chamaecyparis lawsoniana *'Nana Argentea'*

Below Chamaecyparis lawsoniana *'Pygmy'*

Chamaecyparis nootkatensis
Nootka cypress

This tree grows wild from Alaska to north Oregon. It has a regular, conical habit. The sprays of dull-green foliage, which droop down, are about 8 in (20 cm) long and 1.5 in (4 m) wide. The leaves themselves form fine, pointed, overlapping scales that are rough to the touch. Mature trees may reach 100 ft (30 m), with a branch spread of 10 ft (3 m).

The three cultivars **'Glauca'**, **'Lutea'** and **'Pendula'** all make trees as large as the species. 'Glauca' is coloured a deep sea-green rather than the bluish hue its name suggests. 'Lutea' is more aptly named, being golden-yellow when young but losing this colouring with age. 'Pendula' is an attractive tree with a rather open, conical habit. The lower branches curve upwards, while the higher, shorter branches droop. The dark-green foliage hangs in vertical strings from the branches, giving the impression that the tree has been draped in a luxuriant moss.

'Compacta', as its name suggests, is a smaller cultivar. When young it is an almost spherical bush with dull-green foliage. At ten years old it is 30–40 in (75 cm–1 m) tall, but it slowly develops into a small

columnar tree up to 13 ft (4 m) tall at maturity.

Chamaecyparis obtusa
Hinoki cypress

This species can grow into large trees up to 115 ft (35 m) tall in its native Japan, where it is both an important timber tree and sacred to followers of Shinto. In the wild it has a broad, conical habit, with branches spreading horizontally or rising in fans. The foliage is dark green and scale-like, pressed against the branchlets in whorls of four. The shape of the scales, which are blunt-ended, gives rise to the specific epithet *obtusa*. The species doesn't grow very large outside Japan, and has given rise to a number of dwarf or slow-growing cultivars.

This specimen of Chamaecyparis obtusa *'Nana Aurea' has been grown in shade, and has therefore failed to develop its yellow colour.*

'**Nana**' is often confused with '**Nana Gracilis**'. The former is a flat-topped miniature bush 6-8 in (15-20 cm) tall after ten years, reaching a final height of only 20-24 in (50-60 cm). It carries its rich-green foliage on bowl-shaped branchlets. 'Nana Gracilis' grows much faster, reaching the ultimate height of its smaller relative in ten years, and its own ultimate height of about 13-16 ft (4-5 m) in suitable conditions. The bowl-shaped sprays are larger in this cultivar. It forms a more up-right, irregular shrub with age.

To this group may be added the yellow-foliage cultivar '**Nana Lutea**'. This shares the habit of 'Nana Gracilis', but is much smaller, being 8-12 in (20-30 cm) tall after ten years and up to 40 in (1 m) tall at maturity. '**Nana Aurea**' (pictured on the preceding page) is rather smaller, but similar in habit to 'Nana Gracilis'; measuring 12-18 in (30-45 cm) tall after ten years, it reaches an ultimate height of about 5-6 ft (1.5-2 m). The inner foliage is mid-green, while the outer is yellow, but it must be grown in full sun to display this feature.

The *RHS Plant Finder* for 1997-98 lists some 80 cultivars of this species as being available from British nurseries. A diligent search of specialist nurseries will reveal many that are suitable for pot or trough culture, but it is as well to ask a knowledgeable member of staff about how large each of them will grow.

Chamaecyparis pisifera
'Filifera Aurea'

Chamaecyparis pisifera Sawara cypress

This is yet another large, conical tree that can grow to 165 ft (50 m) in its native Japan, where it is cultivated for timber. Like *C. lawsoniana* it has given rise to a large number of cultivars, many of which are dwarfs or slow-growing. Unfortunately none of these plants do well in exposed positions, or in dry and/or alkaline soils. The cultivars may be divided into four categories according to their foliage types (see table).

Adult	Pisifera	Latin = pea-bearing, referring to the small cones of the species
Intermediate	Plumosa	Latin = feathery
Juvenile	Squarrosa	Latin = leaves pointing outwards
Thread-like	Filifera	Latin = thread-bearing

For the smaller garden, the adult foliage forms may be represented by either of the bun-shaped dwarf cultivars 'Compacta' or 'Nana'. Neither of these is likely to exceed 8 in (20 cm) in height after ten years. 'Compacta' has blue-green foliage in tight sprays and a ten-year spread of about 12 in (30 cm). 'Nana' has dark-green foliage, and may be 20 in (50 cm) wide after ten years.

'Snow' is an example of the Plumosa group. It forms a bun-shaped bush, which even in the most ideal conditions is unlikely to exceed 6 ft 6 in (2 m) in height. The foliage is pale green, tipped with white. In addition to acid soil, it requires shelter from strong winds and direct sun, either of which can damage the delicate, chlorophyll-deficient foliage. A semi-shaded spot is best.

'Boulevard' ('Cyano Viridis') is a Squarrosa form, and is one of the most popular garden conifers. It originated as a sport at Boulevard Nursery in the USA in about 1934. It has a roughly conical habit, with feathery sprays of light-blue foliage. To develop its best colour it must be planted in light shade, and in acid soil. At ten years it should be about 6 ft 6 in (2 m) tall and half as wide. Mature trees have been known to reach 20 ft (6 m).

'Squarrosa Sulphurea' may be used either as a lawn specimen or as part of a background planting. After ten years it will form a broadly conical bush

6 ft 6 in (2 m) tall by 40 in (1 m) wide, but it will continue to grow until it is about 13 ft (4 m) tall. As its name suggests, it has the juvenile form of foliage, which is bright sulphur-yellow when it appears in the spring; by winter it turns yellow-green with bronze tips.

'Filifera Aurea' (see left) forms a dense mound of trailing golden whipcord foliage. It should be approximately 40 in (1 m) tall by 60 in (1.5 m) wide ten years after planting, though if it reaches maturity it may be five times as large.

Chamaecyparis thyoides
White cypress

This is another native of the western USA. It is a medium-sized tree that grows to 80 ft (25 m) in the wild. It is capable of growing in swampy ground, but the species and its cultivars dislike shallow, alkaline soils.

Les Andelys in France raised the cultivar 'Andelyensis' ('Leptoclada') about a century ago. It forms a conical tree with dark, bluish-green foliage that bronzes slightly in the winter. It is very slow-growing, reaching a height of just 40 in (1 m) after ten years. One specimen in England has reached a height of 20 ft (6 m). There is an even smaller version — 'Andelyensis Nana' ('Leptoclada Nana') — which has been recorded at 44 in (1.1 m) tall by 35 in (90 cm) wide after 30 years of growth.

'Ericoides' has a compact, conical habit and reaches an

ultimate height of less than 6 ft 6 in (2 m). The dense, juvenile foliage is sea-green in spring and summer, turning bronze or plum-purple in winter. 'Purple Heather' is another cultivar that produces this dramatic winter colour. In this case the spring foliage is grey-green. It is a slow-growing dwarf bush with a bun-shaped habit. 'Heatherbun', 'Red Star' and 'Rubicon' are said to be synonyms of 'Purple Heather'.

Cryptomeria (Taxodiaceae)
Japanese cedar

This genus contains a single species originating from China and Japan, where it is used as a timber tree. The Japanese cedar (*C. japonica*) has also produced many cultivars of different sizes, predominantly from Japan.

The species, which received an AGM in 1993, has a broadly conical shape. It has reached a height of 120 ft (37 m) in the UK, but is taller in its native environment. It prefers moist, acid soils, as do the cultivars. The foliage is in the form of long-pointed, scale-like leaves that point forward at an angle of about 45 degrees to the branchlets. It is bright green, but turns bronze in the winter — a feature shared by many of the cultivars. The cones are roughly spherical, just under 1 in (2.5 cm) in diameter, and have several small spines on each scale.

Cryptomeria japonica *'Globosa Nana'*

foliage is held in flat or irregular drooping sprays. It has been known to reach 100 ft (31 m) in 50 years, and one of the tallest specimens in Britain was measured at 118 × 10 ft (36 × 3 m). The Leyland cypress is very hardy, and can be grown successfully in most conditions, including chalky soils and coastal areas. It is mainly used for tall hedges or windbreaks (see pages 9-10).

'**Bandai-sugi**', which has been awarded the AGM, is a small, slow-growing, irregular bush that will grow to about 40 in (1 m) in ten years. Its unusual growth habit is due to the plant having patches of tight, moss-like foliage among the mature leaves. The foliage is dark green, turning bronze in cold weather.

'**Elegans Compacta**', also an AGM winner, is a slow-growing, broadly conical bush with entirely juvenile foliage that turns a rich purple in winter It is not a true dwarf, reaching 5 ft (1.5 m) in ten years.

'**Globosa Nana**' forms a dense, globe-shaped bush that is about 40-60 in (1-1.5 m) tall after ten years. It carries rich-green adult foliage, arranged spirally around drooping branchlets.

'**Vilmoriniana**' (AGM) is a true dwarf: everything about it

is small. The tiny needles are crowded onto the branchlets, which form a dense, flat-topped dome. The foliage is rich green, turning reddish-purple in winter. At ten years old it is about 16 in (40 cm) tall by 20 in (50 cm) wide. A specimen has been recorded at 24 × 40 in (60 × 100 cm) after 30 years. It is an excellent plant for rock gardens.

× *Cupressocyparis* (Cupressaceae)

These plants are a group of inter-generic hybrids that have all arisen in cultivation.

×*C. lawsoniana* (*Cupressus macrocarpa* × *Chamaecyparis nootkatensis*), the Leyland cypress, is the most important of these hybrids. It is the fastest-growing of all the conifers, and rapidly forms a dense, columnar tree with many steeply rising branches. The

Cupressus (Cupressaceae) Cypresses

Unlike *Chamaecyparis*, where a few species have given rise to a multitude of cultivars, the many species of *Cupressus* have produced relatively few cultivars, with only five species contributing to the list. Many of the species are rare and localised. *The RHS Plant Finder 1997-98* lists just over 40 examples of *Cupressus* as being available in Britain, and eight of those are species.

C. azorica '**Pyramidalis**' (syn. *C. glabra* 'Pyramidalis') is a medium-sized conical tree, suitable for specimen planting in a large garden that can provide a site sheltered from cold winds. As its synonym suggests, it has grey-green foliage. In ten years it should reach a height of 13 ft (4 m), with a spread of 6 ft 6 in (2 m), but its ultimate height will be

Species of *Cupressus*

C. abramsiana (Santa Cruz cypress)
C. arizonica
C. bakeri (Modoc cypress)
C. cashmeriana (Kashmir cypress)
C. corneyana
C. duclouxiana
C. dupreziana
C. forbesii
C. funebris (mourning or Chinese weeping cypress)
C. gigantea
C. glabra (smooth Arizona cypress)
C. goveniana (Gowen cypress)
C. guadalupensis (Tecate cypress)
C. lusitanica
C. lusitanica × *C. macrocarpa*
C. macnabiana (McNab's cypress)
C. macrocarpa (Monterey cypress)
C. sargentii (Sargent's cypress)
C. sempervirens (Italian or Mediterranean cypress)
C. stephensonii (Cuyamaca cypress)
C. torulosa

The Monterey cypress (Cupressus macrocarpa) close to its *locus classicus* at Point Lobos, California. *This specimen shows neither the stature nor the habit of the typical plant, thanks to its unusual growing conditions.*

around 40 ft (12 m). 'Pyramidalis' is an AGM plant. There is a dwarf form — 'Compacta' — which grows to no more than 18 in (45 cm) in ten years.

Among the cultivars of *C. macrocarpa*, there are three notable yellow-foliage clones — **'Donard Gold'**, **'Goldcrest'** and **'Gold Spread'** — that have all been awarded the AGM. Slieve Donard Nursery in Ireland raised the first of them during the 1930s. It has a narrow, columnar habit, with compact, upward-facing branches. Average growth for ten years would be 13 × 5 ft (4 × 1.5 m), though the ultimate height may be about 60 ft (18 m). 'Goldcrest' is very similar, but may be a slightly brighter gold and is also slightly narrower. 'Gold Spread' (syn. 'Horizontalis Aurea') is totally different. It originated in Australia, and is closer in appearance to a 'Pfitzeriana' juniper than a Monterey cypress. At ten years it should have a spread of 10 ft (3 m) and a height of 40 in (1 m). It provides more rapid ground cover than any of the junipers, but you can keep it under control by judicious pruning.

C. sempervirens 'Stricta' has the pencil-slim columnar form that is seen in Italy and other parts of the Mediterranean region. The foliage is dark green. Normally it is 8–10 ft (2.5–3 m) tall and 2 ft 6 in (75 cm) wide. The ultimate height is between 65 ft (20 m) and 80 ft (25 m). There is a slow-growing yellow form raised by Swane Bros Nurseries of New South Wales and called **'Swane's Gold'**. It retains the ultra-slender habit, but at ten years old it is 6 ft 6 in (2 m) tall by 16 in (40 cm) wide. Both these cultivars have been given the AGM. They are rather tender, especially when young, and it is probably not advisable to plant them in the colder parts of the UK.

There is a graceful, weeping conical tree that has been sold as *C. cashmeriana* but is now regarded as *C. torulosa* **'Cashmeriana'**. Another AGM winner, it is of medium size and suitable for planting as a specimen in a large garden. It may be expected to grow to about 16 ft (5 m) tall, with a spread of 6 ft 6 in (2 m), in ten years. Unfortunately it is tender, and should be given some protection against cold winds.

Ginkgo (Ginkgoaceae) Maidenhair tree

This genus contains a single species that is quite unlike the accepted image of a normal conifer. In fact, *G. biloba*, which is a native of China, is the sole primitive survivor of an ancient race.

The maidenhair tree has a short, dull grey trunk, with a network of ridges and fissures on older specimens. The crown is formed by a number of straight, near-upright branches. The most obvious difference from other conifers is in the foliage, which is deciduous (appearing in late April), mid-green in colour and set spirally on short, stout shoots. Each leaf is fan-shaped, ribbed and divided almost into two — hence the specific epithet *biloba*. In October the foliage turns bright yellow, and falls in early November.

G. biloba is hardy, but grows slowly and erratically, especially when young. It forms a medium to large tree, up to 90 ft × 13 ft (28 m × 4 m). It is also very long-lived — the original specimen at Kew is about 250 years old.

The unusual and distinctive leaves of the maidenhair tree (Ginkgo biloba) — a strange 'living fossil' that is quite unlike any other tree.

Juniperus
(Cupressaceae)
Junipers

The genus *Juniperus* includes about 60 species, ranging from prostrate forms to tall trees. Sometimes representatives of several growth habits are present among the cultivars of a single species. Assigning some specimens to the right species is definitely a job for an expert! All are native to some part of the Northern Hemisphere.

The foliage may be the awl-shaped juvenile needles, which can be sharp to the touch, or the triangular adult scale leaves, which lie flat and overlap each other. In some species both types can be present on the same plant. The unifying feature of the junipers is the fact that the fleshy cone scales merge to form a 'berry', which is green at first and ripens to an attractive glaucous blue.

The many juniper species and cultivars form an extremely valuable genus for gardeners.

Species of *Juniperus*

J. ashel
J. californica (Californian juniper)
J. cedrus (Canary Island juniper)
J. chinensis (Chinese juniper)
J. communis (common juniper)
J. conferta (shore juniper)
J. davurica
J. deppeana (chequer-barked or alligator juniper)
J. distana
J. drupacea (Syrian juniper)
J. excelsa (Greek juniper)
J. flaccida (Mexican juniper)
J. formosana (prickly cypress)
J. horizontalis (creeping juniper)
J. indica
J. monosperma (cherry-stone juniper)
J. morrisonicola (Mount Morrison juniper)
J. osteosperma (Utah juniper)
J. oxycedrus (prickly juniper)
J. × pfitzeriana (*J. × media*; *J. chinensis × J. sabina*)
J. phoenicea (Phoenician juniper)
J. pinchotii (red berry juniper)
J. pingii
J. procera (East African juniper)
J. procumbens (creeping juniper)
J. recurva (drooping juniper)
J. rigida (temple juniper)
J. sabina (savin)
J. sargentii
J. scopulorum (Rocky Mountain juniper)
J. sillicicola
J. squamata (flaky juniper)
J. taxifolia
J. thurifera (Spanish juniper)
J. virginiana (pencil cedar)
J. wallichiana

Juniperus cultivars that have been granted an Award of Garden Merit

J. chinensis 'Aurea'
J. chinensis (*J. × media*) 'Blaauw'
J. chinensis 'Kaizuka'
J. chinensis 'Obelisk'
J. chinensis (*J. × media*) 'Plumosa Aurea'
J. chinensis 'Pyramidalis'

J. communis 'Compressa'
J. communis 'Green Carpet'

J. communis 'Hibernica'
J. communis 'Hornibrookii'
J. communis 'Repanda'

J. horizontalis 'Plumosa'
J. horizontalis 'Wiltonii'

J. × pfitzeriana 'Old Gold'
J. × pfitzeriana 'Pfitzeriana'
J. × pfitzeriana 'Pfitzeriana Compacta'

J. procumbens 'Nana'

J. scopulorum 'Blue Heaven'

J. squamata 'Blue Carpet'
J. squamata 'Blue Star'
J. squamata 'Holger'

J. virginiana 'Grey Owl'
J. virginiana 'Sulphur Spray'

Among their numbers can be found plants of many sizes, including representatives of almost all the conifer growth habits; there are colours from greens to yellows, and dark blue-green to silver blue. Most junipers are hardy, and they are tolerant of a wide range of soil types, including thin and chalky. As a result of these virtues, nursery growers are currently offering almost 200 types in the UK. With such riches on offer, it is hardly surprising that only a few of them can be mentioned here. You are therefore recommended to explore the junipers more thoroughly for yourself.

Juniperus chinensis
Chinese juniper

Of the six award-winning cultivars (see the table on the previous page), **'Aurea'**, **'Obelisk'** and **'Pyramidalis'** are conical trees, reaching heights of 6–10 ft (2–3 m) in ten years, with spreads of about 30 in (75 cm). At maturity they may be 20 ft (6 m) tall.

Two further cultivars, **'Blaauw'** and **'Plumosa Aurea'**, were formerly placed in *J.* × *media*, which has since been reclassified as *J.* × *pfitzeriana*! These plants share the rather open, semi-prostrate habit of that hybrid, though 'Blaauw' has strongly ascending branches and eventually develops into a broad, irregular tree. Both have an ultimate

height of 10–13 ft (3–4 m). 'Plumosa Aurea' is as broad as it is tall, but 'Blaauw' may be narrower.

The last AGM cultivar, **'Kaizuka'** ('Torulosa'), has a distinct and unusual habit that gives it an oriental appearance. It has mid-green mature foliage. Its ultimate height is in excess of 10 ft (3 m) and its spread will then be over 13 ft (4 m). It is widely grown in California, where it is often used for landscaping. This has given it the vernacular name of Hollywood juniper. It will also succeed in much colder areas, but will grow more slowly.

Juniperus communis
Common juniper

It is well worth finding a site in the sun for **'Depressa Aurea'**. As its name suggests, it is a low-growing plant with yellow foliage that is brightest in the

spring, when the new growth forms as drooping branchlets of intense butter-yellow juvenile foliage. These turn upwards in the autumn as the plant begins to take on its winter hue of dull bronze. After ten years it is likely to be about 4 ft (1.2 m) in diameter and 1 ft (30 cm) tall, but it will continue to grow, forming a low mound over 10 ft (3 m) across.

'Repanda' is a more vigorous cultivar with mid-green foliage — again this is juvenile, but soft to the touch. After ten years it is about 6 ft 6 in (2 m) in diameter and 10 in (25 cm) above the ground. Thereafter it increases a little in height, and ultimately forms a low mound more than 15 ft (4.5 m) across.

'Hornibrookii', like the other prostrate forms, has branches that follow the ground, and will droop down over a rock or wall. The leaves

Juniperus chinensis *'Kaizuka'*

Juniperus communis *'Gold Cone'*

This close-up of Juniperus communis *'Compressa' shows both the miniature foliage and a reversion to the normal-size needles. Reversions should be cut out of cultivars of all plants as soon as they are found. The only exception is when they seem to offer a worthwhile addition to the range of plants.*

are short and prickly. They tend to twist, revealing their white stomatic bands. This gives the plant a silvery sheen over the grey-green foliage. The plant reaches a spread of about 4 ft (1.2 m) in ten years, when the height is less than 1 ft (30 cm). After this the rate of spread slows down and the plant begins to grow upwards, so that young and mature plants look rather different.

The pencil-slim, dark-green, pointed-columnar cultivar **'Hibernica'**, the Irish juniper, came from Scandinavia in the mid-19th century. The juvenile foliage points upwards on upward, close-growing branches. At ten years old it is 6 ft 6 in (2 m) tall but only 1 ft (30 cm) in diameter. It will finally achieve a height of 25 ft (8 m) and a width of 2 ft (60 cm). **'Crackovia'** is a similar cultivar from Poland. **'Suecica'** is slightly broader, with branch tips that arch outwards.

There is a recent introduction that has the habit of 'Hibernica' but features yellow foliage. It is called **'Gold Cone'**. It is slower-growing than the green forms and is slightly tender, requiring some shelter.

Most people are familiar with another little gem that looks like a miniature Irish juniper, even if they don't know the correct name for it. It's often called the Noah's Ark tree, but it is more correctly known as the cultivar **'Compressa'**. It is slow-growing, even the mid-green needles are miniature,

The creeping juniper (Juniperus horizontalis) *lives up to its name.*

Juniperus horizontalis Creeping juniper

This plant hails from America. The branches, covered in dark, often blue-green adult foliage, are like whipcords. As the name suggests, they hug the ground. Most plants are slow-growing and tend to need careful pruning to produce compact growth. It is difficult to give precise details of spreads, since this species frequently roots down on its runners.

There are many cultivars, but some of them are very similar to each other. **'Plumosa'** has a distinct habit, with branches that grow up at an angle of 45 degrees, causing the plant to reach a height of 20 in (50 cm) — roughly three times taller than most cultivars — while still remaining prostrate!

Juniperus × *pfitzeriana* (*J.* × *media*)

Most cultivars of this hybrid will eventually grow too large for the smaller garden. They may look like the ideal plant for hiding an oil tank or covering an unsightly manhole, but can be dangerous if you plant them too close to structures and underground services.

'Old Gold' may grow to a height of 40 in (1 m) in ten years with a spread of some 5 ft (1.5 m). However, it will then continue to grow, reaching a spread of 10 ft (3 m) and a height of 6 ft 6 in (2 m).

and it seldom grows taller than 40 in (1 m). Its small size makes it suitable for many garden situations — rock gardens, heather beds, sinks, troughs and window boxes.

Juniperus conferta Shore juniper

This species is a most worthwhile garden plant. It has all juvenile foliage that is apple green. It should be planted in full sun and appreciates a moist soil. Though it builds to a low mound in the centre, the outer branches hug the ground and will trail down over rocks or walls. You can expect it to spread to 6 ft 6 in (2 m) in ten years. Left to its own devices it can cover about 16 ft (5 m).

Juniperus × pfitzeriana, *previously called* J. × media, *tends to grow rather too large for a small garden.*

The cultivar **'Pfitzeriana'** may be seen with a spread of 16 ft 6 in (5 m) and a height of 10 ft (3 m). **'Pfitzeriana Compacta'** is smaller, and gives the impression of being more upright because of its more restricted spread. At ten years it should be no more than 40 in (1 m) tall and wide. The upward-arching branches may be steeper than those of 'Pfitzeriana', and the difference is also noticeable in younger plants, which have a higher proportion of juvenile foliage.

Juniperus procumbens
Creeping juniper

The cultivar **'Nana'** has small, close-packed needles of striking mid-green immature foliage. The tips of the branches are upraised. At ten years old it may have a spread of about 5-6 ft (1.5-2 m), and left to its own devices it may extend to 10-13 ft (3-4 m), but it will never grow to more than 6 in (15 cm) in height. You can control the growth by trimming it, but it doesn't have the reputation of crowding out other plants. All in all, this appears to be a good ground-cover plant for small gardens or other restricted spaces.

Juniperus sabina
Savin

The cultivar **'Tamariscifolia'** is of particular interest to gardeners. The species comes from the mountains of central and southern Europe. The plant was described in 1542 in Leonard Fuchs' *De Historia Stirpium*, where it is depicted in a woodcut.

This is a semi-prostrate plant, with dense, grey-blue juvenile foliage. At ten years old it is just 8 in (20 cm) high with a spread of about 40 in (1 m), but it builds up with age to reach an ultimate height of 3 ft (90 cm) with a spread of 13 ft (4 m).

Juniperus scopulorum
Rocky Mountain juniper
This juniper is a small, conical, cypress-like tree with a rather open habit. It has given rise to a number of excellent cultivars. Most of them share the habit of the species, and have silver-blue to steel-blue adult foliage. Although it is possible to root cuttings from *J. scopulorum*, they tend to be short-lived, and it is usual to raise these trees by grafting.

The cultivar **'Blue Heaven'** has foliage of an intense silver-blue — every bit as striking as that of the best blue spruce,

Juniperus squamata *'Blue Star'*

yet more delicate as a result of the thinner branchlets. At five years old it is 40 in (1 m) tall and 12 in (30 cm) wide, and its ultimate height is in the region of 33 ft (10 m). This tree is surely a better choice for a small garden than *Cedrus atlantica* 'Glauca'.

The well-known cultivar **'Sky Rocket'** is aptly named, with its fast-growing blue-grey columnar spire. This cultivar can reach 25 ft (7.5 m) in height, though some plants are slimmer than others.

J. squamata
Flaky juniper
J. squamata has given us some fine garden cultivars, and one

of the best is **'Blue Star'**. This slow-growing, compact, irregular little bush is covered in rather large needles of juvenile foliage. It is thought to require a little shade to develop its most intense colour. After ten years it measures 15 × 18 in (38 × 45 cm), and when fully grown it is unlikely to exceed 40 in (1 m) in height, so there is room for it in any garden.

The same cannot be said for **'Blue Carpet'**. Its foliage is identical to that of 'Blue Star', but it is a rampant spreader, ultimately reaching a span of about 16 ft (5m) and a height of 2 ft (60 cm).

'Holger' is a comparatively recent introduction, so it is not

yet possible to give a reliable estimate of its final size. It is semi-prostrate, and appears to be slow-growing. The foliage is perhaps a little less blue than that of 'Blue Carpet' and 'Blue Star', but the new tips in the spring are yellow.

Juniperus virginiana **Pencil cedar**

Just two cultivars of the pencil cedar have been awarded an AGM. The first of these, **'Grey Owl'**, is a useful ground-cover plant that is equally at home in sun or in shade. The grey-green foliage is mostly adult, and is carried on whipcord branches. At ten years old the plant measures about 12–16 in (30–40 cm) tall and anything up to 8 ft (2.5 m) wide. It can grow on to reach 5 ft × 16 ft 6 in (1.5 × 5 m).

The branches of **'Sulphur Spray'** (the other AGM winner) grow at more of an angle to the ground than those of 'Grey Owl'. The foliage is a soft sulphur-yellow whether in sun or in shade, providing a useful colour break if you plant it among other conifers. The ultimate size of this cultivar should be about 6 ft 6 in × 10 ft (2 × 3 m).

Another useful cultivar is **'Burkii'**. This is a medium-sized columnar tree with a dense habit, clothed in blue-grey foliage — juvenile *and* adult. After ten years it is about 8 ft (2.5 m) tall, and can eventually reach a height of 16 ft 6 in (5 m).

Above Juniperus virginiana *'Grey Owl'*

Below Juniperus virginiana *'Sulphur Spray'*

Larix (Pinaceae)
Larches

The larches are a small group of deciduous species. Most are fast-growing. They are probably of more importance as a timber tree than as garden specimens. However, the names of some cultivars of the Japanese larch *(L. kaempferi)* — 'Bambino', 'Blue Ball', 'Blue Dwarf', 'Little Blue Star', 'Nana', 'Nana Prostrata' — suggest that these at least may be small.

Species of *Larix*

L. decidua (European or common larch)

L. × eurolepis (*L. decidua* × *L. kaempferi*; Dunkeld larch)

L. gmelini (Dahurian larch)

L. griffithsiana (Himalayan larch)

L. kaempferi (Japanese larch)

L. laricina (tamarack)

L. lyallii

L. occidentalis (western larch)

L. × pendula (weeping larch)

L. potaninii (Chinese larch)

L. sibirica (Siberian larch)

This 12-year-old specimen of Larix decidua *may reach an ultimate height of 50 ft (15 m) or more.*

Metasequoia (Taxodiaceae)
Dawn redwood

This genus contains only one species, discovered in central China as recently as 1941. The dawn redwood *(M. glyptostroboides)* reached the UK in 1948, and has been widely planted in parks and large gardens. It is hardy and fast-growing — one specimen has already topped 100 ft (30 m). The habit is rather open and broadly conical. The trunk is ridged and reddish brown. The leaves are linear and borne on deciduous branchlets in two opposite rows, which gives the appearance of a feathery pinnate leaf. It comes into leaf in March. The foliage is larch-green at first, but soon darkens. The leaves turn yellow in October, and then pass through several shades of red before they fall in November.

Picea (Pinaceae)
Spruces

The spruces are a group of about 35 species from the temperate regions of the Northern Hemisphere, especially eastern Asia. They are often conical trees, carrying their branches in whorls. The needles form spirals around the branchlets, or in two lines along them.

At first glance the spruces appear similar to *Abies* (silver firs). However, *Picea* can be clearly distinguished by their pendulous cones (see picture) and peg-like leaf scars.

The genus contains examples of several different growth habits. Like other conifer genera it has produced a number of dwarf or slow-growing cultivars, especially from the species *P. abies*. The genus has

The cones of Picea pungens

Species of *Picea*

P. abies (common or Norway spruce)

P. asperta

P. bicolor

P. brachytyla

P. breweriana (Brewer's weeping spruce)

P. engelmannii (Engelmann's spruce)

P. glauca (white spruce)

P. glehnii (Sakhalin spruce)

P. × *hurtii* (*P. engelmannii* × *P. pungens*)

P. jezoensis (Yezo spruce)

P. koyamae

P. likiangensis

P. × *lutzii* (*P. glauca* × *P. sitchensis*)

P. mariana (black spruce)

P. × *mariorika* (*P. mariana* × *P. ormorika*)

P. maximowiczii

P. morrisonicola

P. obovata (Siberian spruce)

P. omorika (Serbian spruce)

P. orientalis (oriental spruce)

P. polita (tiger-tail spruce)

P. pungens (Colorado spruce)

P. purpurea

P. rubens (red spruce)

P. schrenkiana (Schrenk's spruce)

P. sitchensis (Sitka spruce)

P. smithiana (West Himalayan spruce)

P. spinulosa

P. wilsonii

produced some popular garden subjects. On the other hand, spruces will not thrive in thin or alkaline soils, and they are not particularly hardy.

P. abies 'Little Gem' is a slow-growing, bun-shaped plant with dense foliage. After ten years it is about 12 in (30 cm) in both height and diameter. The ultimate height may be twice that figure, but the width may increase to 40 in (1 m).

P. abies 'Nidiformis' shares the dwarf habit, but it spreads a little wider, making a flat-

***Picea* species and cultivars that have received an AGM**

P. abies 'Little Gem'
P. abies 'Nidiformis'

P. breweriana

P. glauca var. *albertiana* 'Conica'
P. glauca 'Echiniformis'

P. mariana 'Nana'

P. omorika
P. omorika 'Pendula'

P. orientalis
P. orientalis 'Aurea'

P. pungens 'Globosa'
P. pungens 'Hoopsii'
P. pungens 'Koster'
P. pungens 'Procumbens'

P. smithiana

topped bush. After ten years it is 30 in (75 cm) in diameter and one-third of that in height. After 20 years it will spread to 36 in (90 cm), but the height will not be much more than 12 in (30 cm). The new spring growth is apple-green.

To these two dwarfs must be added **P. mariana 'Nana'**, which forms a very tight ball of grey-blue foliage that is at its bluest in summer. At ten years old it is only 3-4 in (8-10 cm) tall, but it grows slowly to a height of 12 in (30 cm) with a spread of 20 in (50 cm).

A mature Picea glauca var. albertiana 'Conica'

P. breweriana is a medium-sized weeping conical tree with dark-green foliage.

P. glauca var. *albertiana* 'Conica' develops into a large, dense, perfectly conical bush of soft grass-green foliage. The ultimate height is between 6 ft 6 in and 10 ft (2–3 m). At ten years old it is much smaller, having reached only 30 in (75 cm) tall by 12 in (30 cm).

P. omorika and its cultivar 'Pendula' are both large trees that should only find homes in the largest of gardens.

A number of *P. pungens* cultivars are popular with many gardeners for their intense blue foliage. *P. pungens* 'Glauca' (blue spruce) should be treated as *Picea pungens* f. *glauca*, including all grey and grey-blue forms, since many plants sold under the cultivar name were raised from seed and were variable.

P. pungens 'Koster' is among the best known of this

Above Picea glauca *var.* albertiana *'Alberta Globe' (in front) — even a mature specimen is dwarfed by* Pinus mugo *'Winter Gold'.*

Right Picea pungens *'Globosa' is equally suited to a small garden.*

group — a medium-sized conical tree with intense powder-blue foliage. At ten years old it is 6 ft 6 in (2 m) tall and half as broad, and will ultimately grow into a 30-ft (9-m) tree with a width of 10 ft (3 m).

P. pungens 'Globosa' is a slow-growing flat-topped bush, 20 in (50 cm) tall and with a spread of 30 in (75 cm) at ten years. It continues to grow beyond that age.

Low-growing forms of the blue spruce, such as *P. pungens* 'Glauca Prostrata' and 'Procumbens', are also available, grown from grafts of side shoots. If they show any sign of developing vertically, you

should prune out the offending shoots immediately.

Pinus (Pinaceae)
Pines

Pinus is a genus of over 100 species, which are distributed throughout the Northern Hemisphere but mainly in the temperate regions.

The leaves are long needles, carried in bunches with two to five needles in each bunch. Young trees are usually conical, possibly to protect their lead shoots from browsing animals. They broaden with age, and tend to become flat-topped, while some discard their lower branches.

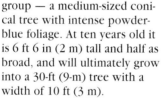

Many pines dislike alkaline soils, whereas others will grow in them quite happily. As a general rule, those with their needles in groups of five resent chalk and lime. Most pines are hardy and will thrive near coasts. However, pines as a whole don't like shade or polluted atmospheres. There are some dwarf and slow-growing cultivars.

Pinus mugo
Mountain pine
This is a very variable species (placing a cultivar in *P. mugo* is a job for an expert), but its needles generally appear in

Species of *Pinus*

P. albicaulis

P. aristata (bristlecone pine)

P. arazonica (Arizona pine)

P. armandii (Armand's pine)

P. attenuata (knobcone pine)

P. ayacahuite (Mexican white pine)

P. banksiana (Jack pine)

P. brutia

P. bungeana (lace-bark pine)

P. canariensis (Canary Island pine)

P. cembra (Arolla pine)

P. caribaea (Caribbean pine)

P. cembroides (Mexican nut pine)

P. chihuahuana

P. contorta (beach pine)

P. coulteri (big-cone pine)

P. culminicola

P. densiflora (Japanese red pine)

P. echinata (short-leaf pine)

P. edulis (two-leaved nut pine)

P. elliottii (slash pine)

P. flexilis (limber pine)

P. gerardiana (Gerard's pine)

P. greggii

P. halepensis (Aleppo pine)

P. hartwegii

P. × holfordiana (P. ayaca-huite var. veitchii × P. wallichiana)

P. × hunnewellii (P. parvi-flora × P. strobus)

P. jeffreyi

P. keslya

P. koraiensis (Korean pine)

P. lambertiana (sugar pine)

P. leiophylla (smooth-leaved pine)

P. leucodermis (Bosnian pine)

P. longaeva

P. luchuensis (Luchu pine)

P. massoniana

P. michoacana

P. monophylla (one-leaved nut pine)

P. montezumae (Montezuma pine)

P. monticola (western white pine)

P. mugo (mountain pine)

P. muricata (bishop pine)

P. nigra (Austrian pine)

P. oaxacana

P. palustris (southern pitch pine)

P. parviflora (Japanese white pine)

P. patula

P. peuce (Macedonian pine)

P. pinaster (maritime pine

P. pinea (umbrella pine)

P. ponderosa (western yellow pine)

P. pseudostrobus

P. pumila (dwarf Siberian pine)

P. pungens (hickory pine)

P. radiata (Monterey pine)

P. resinosa (red pine)

P. rigida (northern pitch pine)

P. roxburghii (long-leaved Indian pine)

P. rudis

P. sabiniana (digger pine)

P. × schwerinii (P. strobus × P. wallichiana)

P. strobus (Weymouth pine)

P. sylvestris (Scots pine)

P. tabuliformis (Chinese pine)

P. taeda (Loblolly pine)

P. taiwanensis

P. thunbergii (black pine)

P. torreyana

P. uncinata (mountain pine)

P. virginiana (scrub pine)

P. wallichiana (Bhutan pine)

P. yunnanensis

Pinus species and cultivars that have received an Award of Garden Merit

P. cembra	*P. nigra*	*P. pinea*
P. coulteri	*P. nigra laricio*	*P. ponderosa*
P. heldreichii var. *leuco-*	*P. nigra laricio* 'Moseri'	*P. pumila* 'Glauca'
dermis	*P. parviflora*	*P. radiata*
P. heldreichii 'Schmidtii'	*P. parviflora* 'Adcock's	*P. strobus* 'Radiata'
P. jeffreyi	Dwarf'	*P. sylvestris*
P. mugo 'Mops'	*P. patula*	*P. sylvestris* 'Aurea'
P. muricata	*P. pinaster*	*P. sylvestris* 'Beuvronensis'

twos. A single photograph cannot show the 'typical' form, but the cultivar **'Winter Gold'**, pictured on page 57, shows the typical habit of many pine species when young. The typical yellow foliage is not evident in the picture, perhaps because it was taken in midsummer.

'Gnom' and **'Mops'** are two well-known slow-growing cultivars. 'Gnom' may be only 30 in (75 cm) in both height and breadth after ten years, but can eventually achieve 6 ft 6 in (2 m). 'Mops' is even smaller, forming a bun-shaped bush 16 in (40 cm) tall by 24 in (60 cm) wide after ten years.

Pinus nigra
Austrian pine
The species is a large tree with a dense habit and an eventual height of up to 130 ft (40 m). Conical when young, it loses its lower branches and takes on a parasol shape with age. The dark-green foliage is of the two-needle type, and this

species will tolerate alkaline soils, cold, and a coastal environment.

The cultivar **'Hornibrooki-ana'** is a slow-growing dwarf, reaching only 2 ft (60 cm) tall and only slightly wider after ten years' growth. But with time it will reach a height and spread of about 6 ft (1.8 m).

Pinus strobus
Weymouth pine
This species is a native of eastern North America — not Dorset, as its vernacular name suggests. Its English name derives from Lord Weymouth's extensive plantings at Longleat in Wiltshire in the early 18th century. One of the five-needle

Pinus nigra *'Hornibrookiana'*

group of pines, it assumes a conical habit when young, but becomes umbrella-shaped when mature.

At about 15 years of age, the cultivar '**Macopin**' is some 15 ft (4.5 m) wide and about

The Weymouth pine (Pinus strobus)

Pinus strobus 'Macopin' shows a growth pattern that is typical of many species of pine.

10 ft (3 m) tall, and appears to be developing a vertical growth habit towards the centre of the bush. This is typical behaviour for many pine species.

Pinus sylvestris
Scots pine

It would not be right to leave this very brief account of some *Pinus* species without a few words about the well-known Scots pine. Its common name belies a range that extends from Spain to Lapland, and east to central Siberia.

The straight trunk and flat-topped canopy are a familiar sight, but the canopy doesn't actually form until vertical growth has ceased — growing trees have a conical habit. The normal lifespan of *P. sylvestris* is about 250 years, although some specimens may reach 400. Full-grown trees can be as much as 115 ft (35 m) tall.

There are dwarf cultivars of *P. sylvestris*, the most popular

Right *A group of mature Scots pines* (Pinus sylvestris)

of these being **'Beuvronensis'**, which originated as a 'witch's broom' on a normal tree. It forms a compact, dome-shaped shrub 24 in (60 cm) tall and 40 in (1 m) across in ten years. It eventually reaches over 6 ft 6 in (2 m) tall and 10 ft (3 m) wide. **'Viridis Compacta'** is an irregular bush of bright-green needles. At ten years it should be about 30 in (75 cm) tall with a spread of 20 in (50 cm), and the 4-in (10-cm) needles give the young plant a rather shaggy appearance. When mature it is 5 ft (1.5 m) tall and 2 ft 6 in (75 cm) wide.

Podocarpus (Podocarpaceae)

This genus consists of 65 or so species, mainly confined to warm temperate and tropical regions of the Southern Hemisphere. Few are hardy, though some succeed in warmer parts of the UK. For this reason, and since proposals have been made to split *Podocarpus* into several genera, the species are not listed here.

P. acutifolius, the New Zealand totara, is capable of growing into a 33-ft (10-m) tree, but you can cultivate it as a shrub by trimming it, and this

also increases the density of the foliage. It makes a good prickly hedge in a warm area. The foliage colour is light olive-green in summer, turning bronze in winter.

P. andinus, the plum-fruited yew, has now been reclassified in the genus *Prumnopitys*. It is a native of the Chilean Andes — yet, despite growing at altitudes of 3,900–6,600 ft (1,200–2,000 m), it is not fully hardy in Britain. If left untrimmed, it becomes a 65-ft (20-m) tree in about 50–60 years. The foliage (see below) is bright green above, but is twisted to reveal the glaucous undersides.

P. macrophyllus is characterised by large yew-like leaves. Like other *Podocarpus* species, it responds well to clipping, so its ultimate size is pretty much up to you.

P. nivalis, the alpine totara, is a low-growing, near-prostrate shrub from New Zealand. It has soft olive-green foliage, and makes an annual growth of about 4 in (10 cm). It is slightly hardier than the species mentioned above.

P. totara '**Aureus**' is a fine slow-growing, upright cultivar, with an irregular conical habit and bright-golden foliage. At ten years old it can be over 6 ft 6 in (2 m) tall if left unattended. However, you can trim it for shape and height.

Pseudolarix (Pinaceae) Golden larch

This genus contains just one species, which differs in a few details from *Larix*. The golden larch (*P. amabilis*) forms a medium-sized conical deciduous tree. It requires acid soil, but will resist a certain amount of pollution and is therefore suitable for growing in towns.

Pseudotsuga (Pinaceae) Douglas firs

The Douglas firs may be distinguished from *Abies* by their pendulous cones, and from *Pinus* by their three-lobed cone bracts. *Pseudotsuga* contains few species: *P. japonica*, *P. macrocarpa*, *P. menziesii* (syn. *P. douglasii*, *P. taxifolia*) and *P. sinensis*. Of these four,

P. menziesii, the Oregon Douglas fir, is the largest and most economically important. It has also given rise to all the cultivars that are currently available in the UK. In the wild the Douglas firs form broadly conical medium or large trees.

Among the dwarf cultivars are *P. menziesii* '**Densa**', *P. m.* '**Gotelli's Pendula**' and *P. m.* var. *glauca* '**Fletcheri**'. The first is a flat-topped, dark-green rock-garden subject that grows about 2 in (5 cm) a year, and is therefore not likely to outgrow its space very quickly. The branches, held horizontally, eventually produce a spread of 40 in (1 m). 'Gotelli's Pendula' is a weeping plant that looks good growing down over a rock. It is about 1 ft (30 cm) tall and twice as wide, and grows slightly faster than 'Densa'. *P. m.* var. *glauca* 'Fletcheri' is rather larger, though still wider than it is tall. It has an irregular habit and a flat top. As the name indicates, it has grey-blue foliage. At about 25 years old, one specimen had reached a height of 4 ft 3 in (1.3 m).

Sequoia (Taxodiaceae) Californian or coast redwood

This genus contains just one species, *S. sempervirens*, which is native to the coastal strip of North America, from southern

Left *The distinctive foliage of* Podocarpus andinus

Right *The coast redwood* (Sequoia sempervirens) *in its native California*

FOUNDERS TREE
HEIGHT   346.1 FT.
DIAMETER   12.7 FT.
CIRCUMFERENCE   40.0 FT
HEIGHT TO LOWEST LIMB   190.4 FT.

Oregon to just south of Monterey in California. The tree has a conical habit, and the lower branches are retained except where trees are grown close together. The trunk is dark reddish-brown and covered with soft, very thick, fissured bark. The leaves are linear and carried in two flat rows along the side shoots. Often, when a large tree is felled, several new ones shoot in a ring from the bole. *S. sempervirens* can live for 2,600 years, but it is rare to find trees much more than 1,000 years old. Having reached a maximum height of 369 ft (112.4 m), it is the tallest tree in the world. Specimens in Scotland have reached as much as 138 × 23 ft (42 × 7 m).

Strangely enough there are creeping cultivars of this huge tree — **'Prostrata'** and **'Nana Pendula'**. **'Adpressa'** is a slow-growing form that grows to between 40 in and 6 ft 6 in (1–2 m) in ten years. Any strong leaders that develop should be pruned back to maintain a dense bush with cream-tipped foliage. Ultimately it will attain a height of up to 33 ft (10 m).

Sequoiadendron (Taxodiaceae) Big tree

The common English name 'Wellingtonia' is wrong, as that name belongs to an altogether smaller plant in another genus. Despite having been introduced into Britain in 1853, *Sequoiadendron giganteum* will always be associated with the 'Iron Duke' in the minds of the British public. It is the only representative of the genus.

This magnificent specimen of Sequoiadendron giganteum is to be found in Windsor Great Park.

Taxodium distichum

In the wild, the big tree is limited to the Sierra Nevada of California, where it grows only at altitudes of 5,000–8,000 ft (1,500–2,500 m). It develops a narrow conical crown unless affected by lightning. The top branches ascend, while those a little lower are level. At first the lower branches droop, but later their tips grow upwards. The lowest remaining branches on the older trees are at a considerable height. The trunk tapers rapidly for the first 40–80 in (1–2 m) and is then cylindrical for much of its height. It is covered with soft, thick, dark-brown bark, with shedding ridges and deep fluting. This serves as a protection against fire — in the wild many trees have extensive fire scars on the windward side. The mature foliage forms hard cords of greyish scale leaves. The dark-green new foliage is made up of sharp-pointed needles, all of them round and at 45 degrees to the branchlets that grow from the older cords.

Sequoiadendron lives for about 3,400 years, and has been known to achieve more than 330 ft (100 m) in height and 90 ft (27 m) in girth. The largest surviving specimens are somewhat smaller, at about 275 × 108 ft (84 × 33 m). Outside the Sierra Nevada, the largest specimens anywhere in the world are in Scotland. One of these has been measured at 168 × 28 ft (51 × 8.5 m).

Taxodium distichum (Taxodiaceae) Swamp cypress

The swamp cypress begins life as a graceful conical tree. At ten years of age it is up to 20 ft (6 m) tall. It eventually develops into a broadly conical tree with a domed top, up to 165 ft (50 m) tall. When mature, the trunk may be twisted and strongly buttressed. It is deciduous, and the apple-green needles, which are set spirally on long shoots, appear in June. In November they turn

65

fox-brown before falling in December. This is one of the best conifers to grow in wet ground, if space is available.

There are two other species of *Taxodium: **T. ascendens*** and ***T. mucronatum***, the Mexican cypress.

Taxus (Taxodiaceae) Yews

Everyone is familiar with the yew as a churchyard tree, a clipped hedge or topiary. In these cases it is usually a dark-green plant, sometimes with red berries. Most people also know it in gardens, where it may be a tree or shrub, upright or prostrate, green or gold.

T. baccata, the common yew, starts as a conical bush, and if left unattended it will grow slowly into a rounded bush on a short trunk. It lives for up to 2,000 years and may reach a height of between 33 ft (10 m) and 80 ft (25 m). Some

Above *This dwarf version of* Taxus baccata *is growing on the Burren near the west coast of Ireland.*

Right Taxus baccata *'Standishii' is a very slow-growing columnar plant, as this 16-year-old specimen demonstrates.*

old yews have remarkable girths of up to 33 ft (10 m). They can be controlled by trimming and are worthwhile as garden plants, as specimens in their own right, or for trimming into hedges or more fanciful shapes.

T. baccata '**Fastigiata**' ('Hibernica'), the Irish yew, offers a more columnar shape. At ten years old it is 6 ft 6 in (2 m) tall and 16 in (40 cm) in diameter. Thereafter the growth may become more rapid, and the conical top may be replaced by a flatter version. There is a similar cultivar with golden foliage called

'**Fastigiata Aurea**', and also a smaller, slower-growing form called '**Standishii**'. The latter shows little tendency to broaden, and a 20-in (50-cm) plant may have taken anything from six to ten years to grow.

There are yews with a spreading habit similar to that of *Juniperus* × *pfitzeriana*. Examples include *T. baccata* '**Cavendishii**' and '**Repandens**'. Each of these may spread to 13 ft (4 m), with a height of 40 in (1 m).

Taller spreading plants may also be found, and it is worth examining the cultivars of *T. cuspidata* and *T.* × *media*.

Thuja (Cupressaceae)

This is a small genus of five species — *T. koraiensis, T. occidentalis, T. orientalis, T. plicata* and *T. standishii* — widely distributed in northern temperate regions. They are hardy evergreen, usually conical trees and shrubs.

Thuja species have provided many useful cultivars in a variety of sizes and colours. They thrive in most soils.

T. occidentalis 'Smaragd' ('Emerald') is a neat, sharply conical tree with close dark-green foliage. At eight years old it is 8 ft (2.5 m) tall by 3 ft (90 cm) wide, so it will probab-

Thuja cultivars that have been granted an AGM

T. occidentalis	*T. orientalis*	*T. plicata*
'Holmstrup'	'Aurea Nana'	'Aurea'
'Lutea Nana'	'Elegantissima'	'Fastigiata'
'Rheingold'		'Irish Gold'
'Smaragd'	*T. plicata*	'Stoneham
	'Atrovirens'	Gold'

ly make quite a large tree. **'Ericoides'** is a low-growing bun-shaped plant. The foliage is purplish-green — a colour similar to that of *Chamaecyparis thyoides* 'Ericoides'. At six years old the plant is about 3 ft (90 cm) wide and 20 in (50 cm) high. **'Globosa'**, as its

name suggests, is roughly spherical. The foliage is a light greyish-green. Its growth rate is average, and it will grow to about 40 in (1 m) in diameter after ten years. **'Rheingold'** is

Thuja orientalis *'Aurea Nana'*

Differentiating the five species of *Thuja*

T. koraiensis: underside almost completely white; smells sweet and lemony.

T. occidentalis: foliage in flattened sprays, underside uniform pale yellowish-green; smells of fruit cake and almonds.

T. orientalis: foliage in vertical sprays, with both sides the same colour; no discernible scent.

T. plicata: smooth, shiny foliage, smelling strongly of pineapple or apple when handled.

T. standishii: hard, dull foliage; no smell until crushed, and then sweet.

a good cultivar that grows broader than it is tall. The foliage is gold in summer, becoming light orange in winter.

T. orientalis 'Aurea Nana' (see previous page) grows slowly to form a dense, globose bush. After ten years it is unlikely to be more than 30 in (75 cm) tall, though ultimately it will reach a height of up to 10 ft (3 m) and a spread of 6 ft (1.8 m).

Another excellent small cultivar is **'Rosedalis'**, which is a roughly spherical bush with soft (entirely juvenile) foliage. In spring it is bright butter-yellow, but by midsummer this has faded to a light green. With the frosts it changes yet again, becoming purple. A fully grown plant is little more than 40 in (1 m) tall.

T. plicata is an important timber tree in North America. It forms a dense conical tree, which may reach almost 200 ft (60 m). It has provided cultivars such as **'Atrovirens'** which are useful for hedging. **'Zebrina'** is a slow-growing, broadly conical tree with golden foliage. At ten years old it will be 10–16 ft (3–4 m) wide, but its eventual height may be as much as 65 ft (20 m). For the smaller garden there is a golden ball cultivar called **'Rogersii'**, which is unlikely ever to exceed 40 in (1 m) in height. **'Stoneham Gold'** is more upright and about twice as tall as 'Rogersii'.

Thujopsis (Cupressaceae)

This genus contains only a single species — *T. dolobrata*. This plant, which is a native of Japan, is closely related to *Thuja*. It has produced a few cultivars, most of which grow into small trees.

Tsuga (Pinaceae) Hemlocks

Tsuga is a genus of about 12 species in all — most of them elegant, broadly conical trees, which are commonly known as hemlocks. They will tolerate shade, and appreciate a moist, loamy soil with good drainage.

Thuja plicata *'Zebrina'*

T. canadensis will tolerate an alkaline soil provided it is not too shallow.

T. canadensis has provided gardeners with a number of dwarf, prostrate or weeping cultivars. **'Nana'** is a slow-growing form of irregular shape with many branches. In ten years it may grow to 30 in (75 cm). **'Jeddeloh'** is a squat bush with lime-green foliage, 40 in (1 m) wide and half as high, while **'Minima'** is a dark-green semi-prostrate bush measuring 40 in (1 m) tall by 10 ft (3 m) wide. **'Pendula'** is weeping form with greyish-green foliage. It requires staking when young. At ten years old it will be 5 ft (1.5 m)

Species of *Tsuga*

T. canadensis (eastern hemlock)

T. caroliniana (Carolina hemlock)

T. chinensis

T. diversifolia (Japanese hemlock)

T. dumosa (Himalayan hemlock)

T. formosana (Taiwan hemlock)

T. forestii

T. heterophylla (western hemlock)

T. × *jeffreyi*

T. mertensiana

T. sieboldii (Japanese hemlock)

T. yunnanensis

tall, and if trained upright it will have the same height — but if left unstaked it will remain prostrate and no more than 2 ft (60 cm) tall. Ultimate-ly it will spread to 30 ft (9 m) across by 10 ft (3 m) tall.

Tsuga canadensis *'Nana'*

Genera, species and some cultivars of heathers

About 2,000 heather cultivars are available, although most of them can only be obtained from specialist nurseries. As with the conifers, there is only sufficient space here to deal with a representative selection. If you need to find out about some of the more unusual cultivars, there are some useful books available — such as the *Handy Guide to Heathers* by David and Anne Small, which gives brief descriptions of a very large number of cultivars.

Andromeda (Arbutoideae) Bog rosemary

This genus contains just two species: *A. polifolia* and *A. latifolia*. It is a low, evergreen shrub, distributed in the cool temperate regions of the Northern Hemisphere from Japan to Europe and Canada. It can be found as far south as the Alps, but towards the southern end of its range it is scarce and confined to high mountains. It is found in northwest England, Ireland, Scotland and Wales.

Bog rosemary grows to about 1 ft (30 cm) in height, in a straggly fashion. Its vernacular name comes from the leaves, which are similar to those of rosemary. They are broadly linear, measuring 0.5-1.5 in

Identifying heathers

As with conifers, it's important to identify these plants accurately in order to be sure of having the ones you really want. So whenever you buy a heather, always check that you have the correct genus, species and cultivar name.

The heathers belong to different subfamilies of the family Ericaceae (see the panel on page 6), so the subfamilies are identified for each genus that is described.

(10-40 mm) long by 2-8 mm wide, dark green and shiny above and silvery-glaucous beneath. The white or pink pitcher-shaped flowers are 5-8 mm long, and held in drooping racemes of two to seven individuals. Most of the cultivars come from Japan.

Bruckenthalia (Ericoideae) Balkan heath

This genus contains just one species — *B. spiculifolia* — which is commonly known as Balkan heath. *Bruckenthalia* is a heather-like dwarf shrub with tiny, dense foliage. The small flowers are displayed above the plant in short, compact racemes measuring 4-6 in (10-15 cm) long

This plant originates from the mountains of Romania and the former Yugoslavia — although its range extends southwards into northern Greece. In Great Britain it flowers between June and July. It is not widely grown, however, and only a very few nurseries offer *Bruckenthalia* for sale.

Calluna (Ericoideae)
Scottish heather or ling

Though *Calluna* contains only one species — *C. vulgaris* — it is distributed all along the western edge of Europe from Norway's North Cape to Morocco, with an excursion into the Mediterranean as far as the northern Balkans.

Calluna is an evergreen shrub between 2 in (5 cm) and 40 in (1 m) tall. The tiny leaves are tightly overlapped on the shoots. In the flower, the calyx lobes are 3-4 mm long, and are as long as, or longer than,

Cultivars of *Calluna vulgaris* that have received an Award of Garden Merit

'Allegro'	'Gold Haze'	'Roland Haagen'
'Annemarie'	'J. H. Hamilton'	'Serlei Aurea'
'Anthony Davis'	'Jimmy Dyce'	'Silver Queen'
'Battle of Arnhem'	'Joy Vanstone'	'Silver Rose'
'Beoley Gold'	'Kinlochruel'	'Sister Anne'
'County Wicklow'	'Mair's Variety'	'Spring Cream'
'Dark Star'	'Mullion'	'Sunset'
'Darkness'	'Orange Queen'	'Tib'
'Elsie Purnell'	'Radnor'	'Underwoodii'
'Finale'	'Red Star'	'White Lawn'
'Firefly'	'Robert Chapman'	'Wickwar Flame'

the corolla. The corolla is lobed, almost to its base. The flowers are held in long, narrow racemes, which are sometimes clustered into panicles. *Calluna* prefers, light acid soils and open situations.

As you might expect in a genus with such a wide distribution, there is considerable variation within it. In 1940, William Beijerinck listed 86 botanical forms and subforms in his monograph *Calluna, the Scotch Heather*. Perhaps he overstated the case, but there is also considerable variation in the cultivars.

Some cultivars such as **'White Lawn'** are ground-hugging forms that grow to no more than 2 in (5 cm) in height. Others like **'White Gown'** are erect and reach a height of some 30 in (75 cm).

Calluna vulgaris *'Allegro'*

The range of foliage colours is impressive, ranging from silver, through every shade of green, to yellow, gold, orange and red. The most intense reds and oranges develop in the winter months, while yet other plants produce cream to red tips on their spring new growth. **'Cream Tips'** and **'Mrs Pat'** are among the cultivars that behave in this way. However, some of the

Left *Young plants of* Calluna vulgaris *'Beoley Silver'*

Below
Calluna vulgaris *'Peter Sparkes'*

greens can look dull in the winter and spring.

Most *Calluna* plants have single flowers and bloom for one or two months. There is also a group in which the stamens have become petaloid, filling the corolla like a minia-ture rose — these are known as double flowers. They are, of course, sterile. As they can't be fertilised, they don't fade for three months or more. **'Peter Sparkes'** is one of this group.

There is yet another group in which the flowers never open fully — the bud bloomers. As with the double-flowered group, they can't be pollinated and don't fade for a long time. They usually begin to show

their colour late in the season, in October, and only start to fade at Christmas. There is a move in the trade to supply these as pot plants to last for one season only. However, like most callunas, they will last for 12 to 15 years in the garden. **'Alexandra'** is an example of a bud bloomer.

In the wild the first plants to flower are those at the north-ern end of their range. The cultivar **'Caekerton White'**, which was collected in Scot-land, blooms from early July to September. **'Heimalis'**, which came originally from the Pyrenees, doesn't open until October and fades in January; this can be a tender plant.

Daboecia cantabrica (Rhododendroideae) St Dabeoc's heath or Irish bell heather

This is an evergreen shrub, usually not much more than 1 ft (30 cm) tall, though it may be achieve more than twice that height when growing through other plants. The species has large, urn-shaped flowers 9–14 mm long, which are carried in lax racemes of three to nine pendant flowers, above the shiny dark-green foliage. The corollas drop when the flowers have been fertilised. The leaves are up to

Daboecia cantabrica *'Alba'*

14 mm long by 5 mm wide, and taper to a point at each end. The underside is silver.

D. cantabrica grows wild in western Ireland, southwestern France, northern Spain and Portugal. In the wild it grows in acid soils, though it can be grown reasonably successfully on neutral soils. It is not totally hardy in a mainland British winter, but if cut back in spring it usually revives. It will tolerate some shade, but should not be grown under trees. It flowers from June to October.

There is a hybrid between *D. cantabrica* and *D. azorica* known as **D. × scotica**. It has a number of cultivars, some of which are very lovely. In the main they are lower-growing than *D. cantabrica*, and for some reason, the hybrid will grow only in acid soils.

Daboecia × scotica *'William Buchanan'*

Daboecia cantabrica *'Cupido'*

Erica arborea *'Estrella Gold'*

Erica (Ericoideae)

All the remaining heathers described in this book belong to the genus *Erica*.

Erica arborea

This plant is usually described as a tree heath, as it can reach 10-16 ft (3-5 m) in sheltered situations in the UK.

E. *arborea* is a native of southern Europe and North Africa, where its range extends from the Atlantic coast of Portugal in the west to Greece and Turkey in the east. In the wild it can be found growing on dolomitic limestone, but it is not as tolerant of alkaline soils as some people seem to imagine.

In British winters E. *arborea* can be tender, but '**Alpina**' is said to be the hardiest cultivar. It has a striking habit of tall, feathery foliage, which requires hard pruning in its early years. It carries small, white, honey-scented, bell-shaped flowers from March to May.

There are two good yellow-foliage cultivars — '**Albert's Gold**' and '**Estrella Gold**' — both of which are slightly smaller than 'Alpina'.

Erica australis

This is another handsome tree heather from Portugal and western Spain. It prefers acid soil, grows to 6 ft 6 in (2 m) and tends to be straggly if it is not pruned at the young stage. In Great Britain it will require protection from cold winds and snow. The flowers, which last from April to June, are 6-9 mm long, tubular to bell-shaped, and showy.

The two outstanding cultivars, both of which have been given AGMs, are '**Mr Robert**', which has white flowers, and '**Riverslea**', which is lilac-pink and close to the normal colour of the wild plant.

Erica carnea
Winter or Alpine heath

E. *carnea*, one of the hardiest of all the heather species, is native to the Alps and the Dolomites, and extends locally southwards to central Italy and Macedonia.

E. *carnea* grows at altitudes of between 2,500 ft (800 m) and 10,000 ft (3,000 m). Since it grows on limestone in the

Erica australis *'Riverslea'*

wild, it will succeed on any garden soil except heavy clay.

This plant seldom reaches more than 8 in (20 cm) in height, though the habit may be compact or spreading. Most cultivars are excellent for ground cover.

The leaves are linear, and may vary in colour from dark bronze-green through apple-green to yellow, orange and red. The flowers are urn-shaped and 0.2–0.3 in (4.5–7.5) mm long. Their colours range from white to a deep red (magenta). The anthers project completely

Erica carnea 'Adrienne Duncan'

Cultivars of _Erica carnea_ that have received an Award of Garden Merit

'Adrienne Duncan'	'Pink Spangles'
'Ann Sparkes'	'Praecox Rubra'
'Challenger'	'R. B. Cooke'
'Foxhollow'	'Springwood White'
'Golden Starlet'	'Sunshine Rambler'
'Loughrigg'	'Vivellii'
'Myretoun Ruby'	'Westwood Yellow'

from the corolla. The flowers begin to open in late November in southern parts of the UK, and though each cultivar blooms for about two months, some will still be flowering into late April.

For a winter display this species is an absolute must, as it remains unbothered by cold winds, ice or snow. Plants covered with snow for weeks on end will still bloom well once the snow has melted.

Even so, you must ensure that you trim it as soon as the flowers fade, since the buds will be set on the new growth by June or July. *E. carnea* cultivars are attractive throughout the year. These plants are widely available, and there is a very good range of cultivars.

Erica ciliaris
Dorset heath

The Dorset heath is native to the Atlantic coast of France, and its range extends from south Brittany down through Spain and Portugal. In the UK it is found only in small areas of Cornwall and Dorset. It grows in moist situations.

E. ciliaris is a dwarf shrub growing up to 3 in (7.5 cm) tall. The leaves are ovate to lanceolate, 0.1-0.2 in (3-6 mm) long, and usually arranged in whorls of three; the white underside is visible. The leaves, pedicels and calyces are covered with long hairs. The corolla is urn-shaped, but sags towards the lower side, and with a length of 0.3-0.5 in (8-12 mm) it is the largest of any native *Erica* species. The anthers don't have awns, and this is the only species with included anthers that lacks them. The flowers are arranged in groups of three, facing in one direction, in terminal racemes up to 4 in (10 cm) long.

In cultivation E. ciliaris will tolerate drier conditions than those it endures in the wild, but it must be grown in acid soil. There are relatively few cultivars, but some of them are well worth growing, flowering between July and late October. They are seldom on offer in garden centres. As with all the hardy ericas, the faded flowers are retained on the plant, so there may be faded flowers, mature flowers and buds all on the same raceme.

Erica ciliaris *'White Wings'*

Erica cinerea
Bell heather

This species grows on the drier parts of heaths and moorland, and in the UK is almost as easy to find as *Calluna vulgaris*. It flowers earlier than *Calluna* — usually in late June. The richness of its colour often makes this plant stand out against the landscape. Bell heather is distributed over most of western Europe, from Norway in the north to northern Italy in the south, and is best suited to acid heathlands.

Erica cinerea is seen here growing in the wild, on the Quantock Hills in the southwest of England.

Cultivars of *Erica cinerea* that have received an Award of Garden Merit

'Alba Minor'	'Hookstone White'
'C. D. Eason'	'Knap Hill Pink'
'C. G. Best'	'P. S. Patrick'
'Cevennes'	'Pentreath'
'Cindy'	'Pink Ice'
'Eden Valley'	'Stephen Davis'
'Fiddler's Gold'	'Velvet Night'
'Golden Hue'	'Windlebrook'

The list of cultivars is very extensive, and the range of flower and foliage colours is much wider than those normally seen in the wild. Unfortunately, however, the cultivars are seldom available from garden centres.

The species is a dwarf evergreen shrub that grows up to 30 in (75 cm) tall. The short leaves are linear and arranged

in whorls of three, and the edges are so tightly rolled that the under-surface is not visible. The corolla is urn-shaped and 4–7 mm long. The anthers are included.

Erica × darleyensis (E. carnea × E. erigena)

This hybrid has occurred in cultivation. It forms a rounded bush, usually up to 2 ft (60 cm) tall and 40 in (1 m) across. The flowers are rather like those of *E. carnea*. Of all the heathers it is probably the easiest to grow. The plants have natural vigour and produce long flower spikes — 8–10 in (20–25 cm) long in some cultivars.

Like both its parents, *E. × darleysensis* is lime-tolerant and will thrive on any soil except clay.

The flowering period is from late November to late April. Some cultivars remain in bloom for the whole of that time without any noticeable fading. An added bonus is the highly coloured new growth on some cultivars. Like its parent *E. carnea*, this hybrid should be trimmed as soon as the flowers fade, and certainly no later than early May.

There are fewer cultivars than in some species, but many are well worth growing. They are widely available.

In the centre of this picture are three Erica × darleyensis *cultivars: 'White Glow', 'Jenny Porter' (pale pink) and 'Arthur Johnson' (tall, mid-pink).*

Erica erigena (E. mediterranea, E. hibernica)

This plant is native to parts of western Ireland (hence the synonym *E. hibernica*), south-west France, Spain and Portugal, but not the Mediterranean. It is a shrub that can grow more than 6 ft 6 in (2 m) tall. The flowers are similar to those of *E. carnea*, to which it is closely related. It is found in moist situations, often growing

79

Erica erigena *'Ewan Jones' on the left is flanked by* E. scoparia azorica *and* Juniperus scopulorum *'Blue Heaven'.*

Erica lusitanica
Portuguese heath

This is one of the loveliest tree heaths for spring flowers. It is native to Portugal, Spain and southwestern France, and has naturalised in parts of southwest England, where it flowers as early as Christmas.

Portuguese heath forms bushes up to 8 ft (2.5 m) tall, with feathery foliage and small, bell-shaped flowers in long, dense racemes. It should be pruned well in its early years, and this is best done immediately after the flowers fade.

E. lusitanica is not fully hardy in the UK, but will grow on most soils, including those that are alkaline. The buds are pink, opening to white flowers, which produces a very attractive effect.

The gold-foliage cultivar **'George Hunt'** is more tender than the species plant, and will need full sun and shelter from the coldest winds.

Erica mackaiana

A scarce species in the wild, *E. mackaiana* is found only in small areas in the bogs of Connemara in western Ireland, and in northwest and southwest Spain.

E. mackaiana is closely related to the more widespread *E. tetralix,* from which it may be distinguished by the

along stream banks or by lough sides. It is lime-tolerant but not totally hardy. The stems are brittle, and can be split by severe frosts. If this occurs, the wood can be cut to 8-10 in (20-25 cm) above ground level, and the plant will usually regenerate to form a good bushy growth.

Many of the cultivars are well worth growing, with blooming periods between November and May. Most of them are spring-flowering. The compact forms of **'W. T. Rackliff'** and **'Golden Lady'** are particularly lovely, as are the taller cultivars such as **'Brian Proudley'** and **'Superba'**. These plants do well in British winters provided they can be given some shelter from the coldest east and northeast winds.

Light', and the magenta-flowered **'Plena'**. The last-named is the only true double-flowered *Erica*; the flowers shade from dark pink to near white, and look like enchanting miniature roses.

Erica manipuliflora

This species isn't, as yet, widely grown, but it's well worth more attention. It is native to the eastern Mediterranean, with a range that extends from the Adriatic through the Aegean to Turkey and Cyprus.

E. manipuliflora is closely related to our native Cornish heath, *E. vagans,* with which it has hybridised — but it is more lime-tolerant and more variable in habit. The bell-shaped flowers are borne on long, narrow, interrupted racemes or, on older plants, short terminal clusters. They have a strong aniseed scent.

In Britain this plant flowers from August to November, but

Above Erica lusitanica *'George Hunt' is more tender even than the species, and will need plenty of sun and shelter.*

Right Erica mackaiana *in close-up*

horizontal whorls of leaves reaching up to the terminal umbels of flowers.

The list of cultivars is short and the plants are not widely available, but if you have acid soil it's worth seeking them out. Especially recommended are the white-flowered **'Dr Ronald Grey'** and **'Shining**

81

Erica manipuliflora *'Aldeburgh'*

'Valerie Griffiths' was a deliberate hybrid between *E. vagans* 'Valerie Proudley' and *E. manipuliflora* 'Aldeburgh'.

'Heaven Scent' was a fortuitous cross that probably occurred in a botanic garden in the early 1950s. It has grey-green foliage and mid-pink flowers, and was named for its particularly strong perfume.

Both of these cultivars form bushes up to 40 in (1 m) tall, each with typical hybrid vigour. They would make an excellent low decorative hedge.

Erica multiflora
This species is the third member of the *E. manipuliflora* and *E. vagans* group. It is native to the Mediterranean as far east as the former Yugoslavia, and grows on alkaline soils. It forms erect bushes, usually up to 30 in (75 mm) tall, although they can reach 8 ft (2.5 m). It flowers from November to February.

This plant is unfortunately not very hardy, and is therefore seldom grown in the UK. It can, however, survive in the southwest of England.

Erica × oldenburgensis (E. arborea × E. carnea)
This cultivated hybrid is a recent introduction from Germany that deserves to become very much more widely known.

in the wild there is evidence that it can continue blooming right through the winter. There is a good variety of flower colours available, ranging from white to rosy purple.

Most cultivars are extremely hardy. The majority of them form dense bushes up to 40 in (1 m) in height, though some weep and trail.

Erica × griffithsii (E. manipuliflora × E. vagans)
Two excellent cultivars of this hybrid are already available, and it is to be hoped that more of them will follow. They are in fact indistinguishable from the best *E. manipuliflora* cultivars, but begin to flower almost a month earlier.

Erica × griffithsii *'Heaven Scent'*

The foliage is feathery, like that of its parent *E. arborea*, but the plants cover the ground well, as do those of its other parent *E. carnea*. The flowers are similar to those of *E. carnea*, but are carried in long, plume-like racemes as on *E. arborea*. It flowers from February to April. Like many *Erica* hybrids, its new growth displays spectacular colours.

Early trials suggest it will be hardy, and more lime-tolerant than *E. arborea*. The authors' own specimen has reached a height of just over 1 ft (30 cm), but will ultimately make a bush about 40 in (1 m) tall. Supplies are very limited at the moment, but there are current-ly two cultivars: **'Ammerland'** with pale pink flowers and **'Oldenburg'** with white.

Erica scoparia
Besom heath

This is a native of southwest Europe, with a range extending as far east as west-central Italy and north to north-central France. It is also found on the Balearic Islands, Corsica and Sardinia, and there are sub-species on the Atlantic islands of Madeira and the Azores.

E. scoparia is not often grown in gardens. It is a slen-der, erect shrub that can grow to 20 ft (6 m) in the Azores, but nearer to 40 in (1 m) in Europe. Its rather feathery foliage is carried in attractive whorls in the case of the Azores subspecies (see picture on page 80). The flowers are insignificant — just 3 mm long, greenish brown, and almost hidden in the leaf axils.

Erica × stuartii
(E. × praegeri)

This is a naturally occurring hybrid between *E. mackaiana* and *E. tetralix*, found only in Ireland, where its seed parent is present. It is not found in the *E. mackaiana* stations in Spain. It flowers from May to November, and for most of the year it is difficult to distinguish it from its parents. In spring, however, its new growth

shows the characteristic bright colours of the hybrid. The cultivars **'Irish Lemon'**, **'Irish Orange'** and **'Pat Turpin'** are worth seeking out for acid soils, but the original plant, **'Stuartii'**, is arguably no more than a curiosity.

A self-set Erica terminalis

Erica terminalis

This species comes from the western Mediterranean, with a range extending from south-west Italy and Corsica to south-west Spain.

E. terminalis is one of the hardiest of all the shrub heathers and has naturalised at one place in Northern Ireland.

It is lime-tolerant and flowers from July to November. The faded flowers, which turn to a russet brown, are carried right through the winter and look very attractive. If pruning is necessary, it is best done in mid-March.

The flowers are pink, but those of the cultivar **'Thelma Woolner'** are rather darker than those of the species. The botanical literature mentions a white form, but this is not in cultivation at present.

Erica tetralix
Cross-leaved heath

This is a widely distributed species, growing in western and northern Europe. Its range extends eastwards as far as Latvia and central Finland, and south to northern Spain and Portugal. It grows in damp, acid environments.

Cross-leaved heath is a straggling dwarf shrub, up to 30 in (75 cm) tall with weak ascending stems. The leaves are lanceolate, up to 6 mm long, and usually carried in whorls of four — hence the vernacular name. Below the flowers they are small and closely pressed to the stem. The stems, leaves and calyces are hairy, giving the plant a grey appearance. The flowers are rather large, with urn-shaped corollas 5–9 mm long completely enclosing the anthers. They are carried in drooping terminal umbels. The flower colour ranges from an opalescent deep pink to white.

The colour is usually deepest on the top of the flowers. The species blooms from June to October.

E. tetralix hybridises, more or less freely, with *E. ciliaris, E. mackaiana, E. vagans* and possibly *E. cinerea*. There is a good range of cultivars, some of them bearing the name of Underwood, a family of nursery growers.

Erica umbellata

This is a moderately tender species from western Spain and Portugal. A shrub up to 30 in (75 cm) tall, it has attractive feathery foliage and mauve flowers from April to June. This plant is not widely grown,

Above Erica tetralix *'Melbury White'*

Right *This close-up of* Erica umbellata *shows the unique constricted flower shape.*

but makes a useful bridge between the last of the spring-flowering and the first of the summer-flowering species. It is said to tolerate alkalinity, but grows naturally only in acid soils. It is reasonably tolerant of drought, and flowers profusely if it is not trimmed.

Erica vagans
Cornish heath

This species is native to the UK, where in the wild it is now limited to the Lizard peninsula. It is also found in Spain, and in

Erica vagans *'Kevernensis Alba'*

southwest France around the town of Narbonne. There is a colony of white-flowered plants of uncertain status in Northern Ireland.

Cornish heath forms a dense bush up to 40 in (1 m) tall. The flowers are small and bell-shaped, with protruding anthers. They are carried in dense, cylindrical racemes, and open progressively from the bottom. During most of the flowering period (from August to late October), faded flowers, newly opened flowers and unopened buds will be present on each raceme. The faded russet flowers are attractive in winter, especially if planted with a white *E. × darleyensis*. Each raceme terminates in a tuft of leaves.

E. vagans will tolerate moderately alkaline soils if there is enough magnesium present. There is a range of good gardenworthy cultivars from white to bright cerise. Some of them have golden foliage. This species is seldom seen in garden centres.

Erica × veitchii (E. arborea × E. lusitanica)
This hybrid occurred fortuitously at Veitch's Nursery in Exeter in about 1911. It was subsequently discovered in the wild on the Iberian peninsular. Recently several new cultivars such as **'Gold Tips'** and **'Pink Joy'** have been added to the limited range.

The hybrid closely resembles its parents in all respects. It is lime-tolerant but relatively tender. Given shelter it can reach 8 ft (2.5 m) in height. It flowers from March to May.

Erica × watsonii
(E. ciliaris × E. tetralix)

Hugh Cotteral Watson found this naturally occurring hybrid on Carrine Common, near Truro in Cornwall, in 1835. It was what is now known as the cultivar **'Truro'**, and it still grows at its *locus classicus*. Most of the other cultivars were found near Wareham in Dorset, and introduced by the local firm of Maxwell & Beale.

The hybrid forms a dome-shaped bush 1 ft (30 cm) or so high. The flowers and their manner of carriage show every intermediate between the parents. This has given rise to the idea of an 'hybrid swarm' formed by back-crossing the hybrid with its parents. In fact,

Erica × watsonii *'H. Maxwell'*

E. × watsonii, like almost all *Erica* hybrids, is almost totally sterile. It is hardy, but requires an acid soil. It blooms from June to October and exhibits the hybrid characteristic of coloured new growth.

Erica × williamsii
(E. tetralix × E. vagans)

This hybrid grows, very rarely, on the Lizard in Cornwall. It was first found in 1860, but was not described until 1911.

The plant forms a dense, erect bush about 2 ft (60 cm) tall and ultimately about 6 ft (2 m) in diameter. The flowers are small, pale pink and urn-shaped — altogether intermediate between those of *E. tetralix* and *E. vagans*. They are present in little clusters from July to November. The

foliage is attractively tipped with yellow new growth. It is hardy, and will grow successfully in neutral or even slightly alkaline soil.

The hybrid probably occurs quite frequently in the wild, but most specimens lack hybrid vigour and do not survive. Dr Griffiths of Leeds bred a fascinating little yellow bun of a plant, no more than 2 in (5 cm) tall by 3 in (7.5 cm) across, which he called 'Gold Button'. Some interesting plants of a more normal size have been bred in western Canada, and we can look forward to them becoming available in the UK. In the meantime, there are a few worthwhile cultivars on offer if you're willing to search hard for them.

Flat sites

Flat sites are certainly easier to work on than sloping sites, but it's more difficult to make them interesting and attractive. The author, in designing her own garden, also had the problem of planning plantings suitable for an alkaline soil with a pH between 8 and 8.3. To begin with, summer-flowering plants were not included in the designs, so foliage colour was the prime consideration for summer colour.

The winter-flowering *Erica carnea* cultivars vary in foliage colour from all shades of green through dark bronze-green to gold and orange. Adding the more blue-green junipers to the scene makes the overall summer effect pleasing, cool and restful. The planting changes dramatically through December and January as the heathers come into bloom. The fullest colour appears from mid-February through to late March. In the north and east of the UK this flowering period would be approximately two to three weeks later.

If you don't want the work and the expense involved in building raised beds, then you can achieve variety in height with careful planting. The tallest-growing plants take time to mature, but it's fun to plan a garden like this, and hugely enjoyable to watch your ideas turning slowly into reality.

Above *A bed planted by the author, showing its summer foliage colours*

Below *The same bed, showing the colours produced by winter flowers*

Small gardens can be made interesting by shaping the beds, by using varied foliage colours as well as flower colours, and by adding paths and grass. If your space is limited, choose the few plants that you can use with great care. They will give you a lot of pleasure. It's usually best to choose foliage colours first, as on evergreen plants these will be visible all year round. You can then regard flower colour as a bonus in season.

Building mounds

If you have a larger area of flat ground, then you may want to try a different form of heather planting that can work very well: building mounds of soil with timber frames to enclose them. The plants (all of a single cultivar) can be planted in tiers, and when they grow together they will give the effect of an undulating landscape.

Borders

Many of us don't have large gardens, but we can still enjoy a good display of plants around the house and along paths and drives. Both conifers and heathers will do well, but always remember that these plants prefer the rain and sun that they receive on south- and west-facing aspects, and don't forget that conditions can be very dry at the foot of a wall.

The foliage colours, height variation and texture of conifers will make a lovely display. They're indispensable for large beds and borders, and some conifers will thrive in shade where heathers would not.

Heathers, too, will give a striking effect for the front of a border, especially when you use taller plants as a backdrop.

Island beds

For heathers, in particular, an island bed in the middle of the lawn may be the sunniest and

Building a mound for a heather garden

A conifer border

This large garden has been laid out with multiple island beds.

most suitable place in the garden. The shape of the bed is a matter of personal choice — though naturally flowing, curved shapes are easier for mowers to negotiate than tight, square corners. In fact, a good way to fix the boundaries of a new bed is by pushing the lawn mower round the proposed curves while the grass is long.

In a large garden you can combine a number of small island beds to create a very pleasing effect. Their size will make weeding and trimming easier, because you'll have access to the centres of the beds from all sides. With larger island beds, you may need to lay paths through the bed for this purpose, using paving slabs set as stepping stones, or coarse bark chippings.

Raised and sloping sites

Raised beds

Raised beds are a good way of displaying your plants. The soil can be contained in a raised bed, and the height you choose can be anything from a lowly 1 ft (30 cm) up to 3 ft (90 cm). Higher raised beds can make gardening possible for disabled people, especially if they're sited next to patios and paths.

Old railway sleepers can look natural, especially when the plants grow over the edges to soften the straight lines. However, felled sapling trees stripped of their branches will do just as well if they're pegged into position.

Building walls for raised beds in brick or stone sets off the plants very well, and if you choose the right materials they will blend attractively with the adjacent buildings. Remember that the roots can get very hot in these beds when the sun shines on the walls. So be sure to water them adequately.

Peat blocks are available in some areas of the country, and experience suggests that they will last for 10 to 15 years. To build a wall, soak the blocks thoroughly and use a 'mortar' made of fine peat mixed with clay between the courses. The wall should be sloped so that

its top is angled towards the soil it is retaining. If you want to set plants on the face of the wall, then plant them between the courses while the wall is being built.

The dark colour of the peat contrasts well with the lighter foliage and flower colours, and

Old railway sleepers can be very useful in the garden.

plants will root into it, giving a very natural effect. Raising the central section of a bed with peat blocks creates a two-tier effect, and will give extra prominence to your plants.

Natural slopes

On a natural slope you may need to build terraces by laying horizontal paths to separate planting areas at different levels. You can also introduce steps, with low plants growing up the sides of them.

The picture below shows a very lovely garden that has been created on a sloping site using bold groups of low-growing heathers. This picture was actually taken in September, but later in the year, when the winter-flowering heathers take over, the display is equally colourful.

Low-growing heathers planted beside steps on a natural slope

Banks

Banks beside a drive, or on a road frontage, look very good indeed when closely planted with conifers or heathers. You'll probably need a low wall to retain the soil.

Again it is possible to achieve an effect throughout the year. The conifers can be set higher up the bank as a backdrop to the heathers, and keeping the heathers at a lower level makes it easier to reach them when they need trimming.

On a very windy and exposed hillside, the dwarf conifers and low-growing heathers will cope well with any really hostile conditions. As long as you choose compact varieties, they should tolerate any amount of rain, snow and wind.

Above *An exposed garden*

Where to see conifers and heathers

A final thought

The design ideas suggested here may help you in planning your garden, but the aspect of your garden, its shape, and the position of existing mature trees, will always control what is possible. You should get a lot of pleasure from planning the layout and choosing the plants — and you'll get even more pleasure from watching your designs mature into a beautiful garden.

National Collections

If you're starting to get interested in conifers and heathers, then it's well worth seeking out the places where the relevant National Collections are being grown. Over the years, some gardeners have pursued a passion for a particular group of plants, and they've collected together large numbers of fine examples of species and cultivars.

The National Council for the Conservation of Plants and Gardens (NCCPG) came into being in 1978 to 'identify and propagate those plants rare or on the verge of extinction in our gardens, to search out and reintroduce those apparently lost …' From this developed the scheme for recognising National Reference Collections which is run by the NCCPG. They have local branches, which can be contacted by writing to this address:

The National Development Officer
NCCPG
The Pines
Wisley Garden
Woking
Surrey
GU23 6QP

The NCCPG also publishes *The National Plant Collections Directory.*

The details of the National Collections of conifers and heathers are as follows:

Conifers

Abies and *Picea*

S. J. Noble
Ardkinglas Estates
Cairndow
Argyll
PA26 8BH

No. of species: *Abies* 33, *Picea* 24

Open by appointment; admission free

Chamaecyparis lawsoniana

Dr R. J. Gornall
Leicester University Botanic Garden
Beaumont Hill
Stoughton Drive South
Oadby
Leicester
LE2 2NA

No. of cultivars: 90

Open Monday to Friday; admission free

Chamaecyparis lawsoniana, × *Cupressocyparis, Juniperus, Taxus, Thuja*

C. Morgan
Bedgebury National Pinetum
Bedgebury
Kent
TN17 2SL

No. of species: *Juniperus* 20, *Taxus* 7, *Thuja* 5

No. of cultivars: *Chamaecyparis lawsoniana* 139, × *Cupressocyparis* 26, *Juniperus* 84, *Taxus* 49, *Thuja* 63

Open daily; admission charge

Dwarf and slow-growing conifers

J. Bond
Saville and Valley Gardens
Windsor Great Park
Windsor
Berks
SL4 2HT

No. of species: 342

No. of cultivars: 2,480

Open daily; admission charge

Pinus
(except dwarf cultivars)

The Curator
Royal Horticultural Society
Garden
Wisley
Woking
Surrey
GU23 6QB

No. of species: 112

No. of cultivars: 43

Open daily; admission charge/
RHS membership

Taxus

P. Brown
University of Bath
Claverton Down
Bath
North Somerset
BA2 7AY

No. of species/cultivars 20

Open daily; admission free

Heathers

Calluna vulgaris

M. R. Shaw
Northern Horticultural Society
Harlow Carr Botanical Gardens
Crag Lane
Harrogate
North Yorks
HG3 1QB

No. of cultivars: 400

Open daily; admission charge/
NHS or RHS membership

Calluna vulgaris, Daboecia, Erica

The Curator
Royal Horticultural Society
Garden
Wisley
Woking
Surrey
GU23 6QB

No. of species: *Erica* 17

No. of cultivars: *Calluna vulgaris* 509, *Daboecia* 46, *Erica* 439

Open daily; admission charge/
RHS membership

Calluna vulgaris, Daboecia, Erica

D. Donoghue
United Distillers
Cherrybank Gardens
Cherrybank
Perth
PH2 0NG

No. of species/cultivars: 1,000

Open 5 May to 13 October;
admission charge

Part of the Wisley Collection

Other information

Part of the United Distillers' Collection

Where to obtain plants

The *RHS Plant Finder* is published annually. It lists approximately 70,000 plants and tells you where you can buy them. It gives names, addresses and telephone numbers of the growers, together with their opening times, the price of their catalogues, and whether they will supply by mail order.

The specialist nurseries are well worth seeking out, as they will not only supply the plants you want, but will give you sound advice and information about the plants.

Books on conifers and heathers

The first two titles are large, comprehensive volumes for the specialist.

Manual of Cultivated Conifers, Gerd Krussmann

Conifers: The Illustrated Encyclopaedia (2 volumes), D. M. van Gelderen and J. R. P. van Hoey Smith

Heathers, Conifers and the Winter Garden, Frank Knight, John Bond, Lyn Randall and Robert Pearson

A Wisley Gardening Companion (also available as three individual handbooks)

Handy Guide to Heathers, David and Anne Small

The last of these gives brief descriptions and sources of supply for over 1,000 heather cultivars, including many of the latest introductions.

There are also several older books which may still be available through public libraries or second-hand dealers (where possible, the date of publication is included):

Ornamental Conifers, C. R. Harrison (1975)

Conifers For Your Garden, Adrian Bloom

Garden Conifers in colour, Brian and Valerie Proudley (1976)

Heathers in colour, Brian and Valerie Proudley (1974)

The Heather Garden, Harry van de Laar (1978)

Heaths and Heathers, Terry Underhill (1990)

The Heather Society

The Heather Society was founded in 1963. Its purpose is 'to assist in the advancement of horticulture and in particular the improvement of and research into the growing of heaths, heathers and associated plants.'

The Society has a world-wide membership at all levels of experience. It provides a friendly and helpful link between members, and organises local events and visits as well as an annual conference. The Society is the International Registration Authority for *Andromeda, Bruckenthalia, Calluna, Daboecia* and *Erica*. Its *Yearbook*, and three bulletins a year, keep members informed on research, new cultivars, cultural experiences, and the Society's activities.

The Society is on the Internet with a home page at:

http://www.users.zetnet.co.uk/heather/

For details of membership, or other enquiries, please contact the Society's Administrator:

Mrs Anne Small
Denbeigh
All Saints Road
Creeting St Mary
Ipswich
Suffolk
IP6 8PJ

Telephone/fax 01449 711220
E-mail heathers@zetnet.co.uk

Index